Protecting Patients at All Costs

The Drug Watch Dogs

By Martin G. Van Trieste

Dedication

I dedicate this book to my lovely wife, Cynthia, and my three beautiful daughters, Jennifer, Susan, and Mary Margaret, who have supported me in my career, put up with several moves across the country and listened to me discuss work at the dinner table.

I also dedicate this book to the patients I had the opportunity to serve from a distance. My work life has been guided by knowing that serving patients is a privilege and that privilege comes with significant responsibilities. Those responsibilities include providing quality drugs that are always available.

While authoring this book, and today, April 10, 2023, I learned that I have kidney cancer and will have a partial nephrectomy (removal of part of one of my kidneys) on July 11, 2023. So, as of today, I am a patient with cancer. This diagnosis will probably impact how I write and edit the book through completion.

About the Author

Martin VanTrieste is a visionary leader and accomplished professional in the fields of pharmaceuticals and healthcare. With a career spanning several decades, VanTrieste has left an indelible mark on the industry through his dedication to innovation, patient safety, and quality assurance.

As a young and driven individual, VanTrieste embarked on his journey by earning a Bachelor's degree in Pharmacy from a prestigious institution. This educational foundation provided him with a strong scientific background that would become instrumental in shaping his later achievements.

VanTrieste's early career was characterized by his commitment to continuous improvement and his passion for ensuring the highest standards in pharmaceutical manufacturing. He rapidly ascended the ranks within reputable companies, showcasing his prowess in regulatory compliance, quality control, and risk management.

Throughout his career, VanTrieste demonstrated a unique ability to navigate complex regulatory landscapes, advocating for stringent quality control measures and driving the implementation of cutting-edge technologies. His forward-thinking approach led to the adoption of innovative practices that significantly enhanced product safety and efficacy.

One of VanTrieste's most notable contributions is his focus on the patient. Recognizing the critical importance of putting patients at the heart of every decision, he spearheaded initiatives to improve communication between healthcare providers, regulatory bodies, and patients. This empathetic approach revolutionized how the industry perceives and serves its ultimate beneficiaries.

In addition to his corporate accomplishments, VanTrieste is a sought-after speaker and thought leader, frequently sharing his insights at international conferences and symposia. His articulate and passionate advocacy for patient safety and pharmaceutical quality has inspired countless professionals to uphold the highest ethical standards.

VanTrieste's impact extends beyond his professional achievements, as he is also a dedicated mentor and philanthropist. He actively engages with aspiring pharmacists and young professionals, nurturing the next generation of leaders and instilling in them the values of integrity, perseverance, and innovation.

Martin VanTrieste's journey is a testament to the power of unwavering dedication, forward-thinking, and a genuine passion for improving the lives of others. His legacy continues to shape the pharmaceutical and healthcare landscape, impacting the industry and the patients it serves.

Chapter 1 - Prologue

Pharmaceuticals have a long and rich history that dates back thousands of years. The earliest recorded use of medicinal plants dates back to ancient civilizations such as the Sumerians, Egyptians, and Chinese, who used various herbs and plants to treat various ailments. These ancient civilizations recognized the therapeutic properties of plants and developed methods for using them in medicine.

The ancient Greeks made significant contributions to the field of pharmacy and pharmacology. Famous figures such as Hippocrates and Galen wrote extensively about the use of drugs and their effects on the human body. Hippocrates is considered the father of modern medicine, and his work laid the foundation for the development of pharmaceuticals. On the other hand, Galen was a physician and philosopher who contributed significantly to understanding anatomy and physiology.

In the Middle Ages, Arabic and Islamic scholars made significant advancements in the field of pharmacy and the use of drugs. They translated many Greek works on medicine into Arabic and expanded upon them, developing new theories and techniques. During this time, the practice of compounding and dispensing drugs became an established profession, and the first pharmacopeia, a compilation of medicinal substances and their uses, was written.

During the 19th century, pharmaceuticals underwent a significant transformation by introducing synthetic drugs and chemical compounds. This transformation allowed for the mass production of drugs and made them more affordable and accessible to the general public.

Additionally, the advent of modern pharmaceuticals led to the development of new treatments for previously untreatable diseases, such as tuberculosis and cholera.

This period also saw the rise of pharmaceutical companies and the development of innovative marketing practices, which helped to increase the public's access to drugs.

The 20th century saw a significant pharmaceutical industry expansion, with modern technologies, regulations, and marketing practices leading to the development of many new drugs. This period also saw the discovery of antibiotics, revolutionizing the treatment of infectious diseases. The discovery of penicillin, for example, led to the development of other antibiotics and paved the way for treating many previously untreatable infections.

It has been said that penicillin, first developed in 1928 by Alexander Fleming, is seen as a miracle drug. It was the first antibiotic and the start of the innovation and advancement of antibiotics. Antibiotics are used to treat and prevent bacterial infections. Individuals started using penicillin on a big scale during WWII. It has been estimated that the drug has saved over 80 million lives and that 75% of the current world population would not exist if it were not for penicillin since one of their ancestors would have died from an infection. These facts are why this drug is one of the, if not the, most crucial drug inventions ever.

The pharmaceutical industry continued to grow and evolve in the latter half of the 20th century, with modern technologies such as molecular biology and genetic engineering leading to new drugs and therapies. This period also saw the rise of biotechnology and the development of biotech pharmaceuticals, drugs produced using living cells.

Today, pharmaceuticals play a crucial role in healthcare, developing new treatments and therapies for a wide range of diseases and conditions. From the treatment of infectious diseases and chronic conditions such as diabetes and heart disease to the management of mental health disorders, pharmaceuticals have become an essential part of modern medicine.

However, the pharmaceutical industry is not without its controversies. The high cost of drugs, particularly in the United States, has become a significant issue in recent years, with many individuals struggling to afford the necessary treatments. Additionally, concerns about the safety and efficacy of some drugs have led to increased scrutiny and regulation of the pharmaceutical industry.

Despite these challenges, the pharmaceutical industry continues to play a crucial role in improving public health and addressing the healthcare needs of individuals worldwide. With ongoing advances in technology and research, the future of pharmaceuticals is bright, and we can expect to see many new and innovative treatments in the years to come.

As science and medicine advance, so must our quality systems to effectively monitor and improve new processes required to support these advancements.

Chapter 2- Introduction

This book exposes patients and consumers to the risks when taking substandard, low-quality or counterfeit drugs and what is required to prevent these risks. It also delves into the daily life of quality executives and the challenges they routinely encounter as they strive to protect patients.

Every day, an army of dedicated individuals work tirelessly to protect patients. Still, as you will read, another army is trying to nullify these efforts to sell substandard and counterfeit drugs to unsuspecting consumers and patients.

Finally, the book gives examples of some of the dangers patients may face, such as human errors during manufacturing, a global network of suppliers, manufacturers, distributors, and wholesalers that may not be reliable, outdated and insufficient manufacturing processes, scarcity of raw materials for essential drugs, counterfeit raw materials and drugs, and other bad actors in the supply chain that may be beyond our control.

Throughout the book, I will try to detail how to build defenses to combat these threats. Every day I went to work, I thought about the next threat and how to defend against it. However, I also recognized that every day, an army of unethical and criminal elements was trying to figure out new ways to avoid my defenses, making the job even harder. Sometimes, the enemy is within the company. A few individuals are always passive-aggressive, lazy, mad at the company, or incapable of doing their jobs. Unfortunately, every individual who doesn't toe the line puts patients at risk.

The job of a pharmaceutical professional and leader is complex and specialized. Even though a great deal of knowledge for a pharmaceutical professional can be obtained via formal education, a vast amount must be acquired through on-the-job training, job experience, and mentoring. Therefore, I hope sharing my experiences will help the next generation succeed.

In general, the role of a pharmaceutical professional is to help ensure that safe and effective drugs are developed, manufactured, and made available to the public while complying with relevant standards and regulations.

A typical day in the life of a quality executive would involve overseeing the implementation of quality control and assurance processes in the organization. This day may involve:

- Most importantly, being vigilant about possible threats and implementing procedures to deal with these threats.
- Conducting regular audits to ensure compliance with quality standards
- Developing and implementing effective and efficient quality policies and procedures
- Analyzing data and customer feedback to identify areas for improvement
- Collaborating with cross-functional teams to resolve quality issues
- Training employees on quality practices and procedures
- Staying current with industry developments and emerging quality trends

- Presenting updates and findings to senior management
- Maintaining relevant certifications and accreditations
- Responding promptly to address events that put patients at risk

The specific tasks and responsibilities of a quality executive may vary depending on the size and nature of the organization.

However, there are crazy and stressful days in the life of a quality executive. As an analogy, a pilot once told me that being a pilot is hours of boredom punctuated by moments of sheer terror. A quality executive could involve unexpected and high-pressure situations such as:

- Responding to an FDA inspection that has uncovered a significant quality issue at a manufacturing facility
- Dealing with a product recall that could impact the company's reputation and financial stability
- Addressing a production issue that could result in a shortage of a life-saving drug
- Managing a crisis that could affect the company's compliance with cGMP regulations
- Conducting an emergency investigation into a manufacturing issue that could impact the safety or potency of a drug
- Implementing contingency plans for a supply chain disruption that could affect the delivery of essential medicines

In the pharmaceutical industry, quality and regulatory compliance are critical. A quality executive must assess the situation quickly, make informed decisions, and resolve the issue while ensuring drug supply, patient safety, and regulatory compliance.

As a quality executive, sometimes you take the brunt of everything that goes wrong. An anonymous author once authored the following poem titled "The Train," which is how I felt on many days at work:

[The Train]

by Anonymous

It's not my job to run the train,
The whistle I don't blow.
It's not my job to say how far
The train's supposed to go.
I'm not allowed to pull the brake,
Or even ring the bell.
But let the damn thing leave the track
And see who catches hell!

I will describe why a quality professional feels this way occasionally, but more importantly, the skills required to control the train's operation!

A successful pharmaceutical quality executive typically possesses a combination of technical, regulatory, and leadership skills.

- Technical skills: Knowledge of pharmaceutical manufacturing and quality control processes and understanding of relevant regulatory guidelines and industry standards.
- Regulatory skills: Knowledge of FDA and other global regulatory requirements and the ability to interpret and implement them in pharmaceutical manufacturing. I have always said that the quality executive must know these requirements better than the regulators.
- Thirst for Knowledge: Staying informed about the latest developments facilitates informed decisions and staying ahead of new technologies and regulations. A desire to learn new things and stay current with changing trends helps improve skills and expand their knowledge base. A thirst for knowledge can inspire creative thinking, developing new and innovative ideas to tackle challenges. Knowledge equips us to analyze complex problems and make informed decisions that benefit the organization.
- Leadership skills: Strong leadership skills, experience managing teams, and the ability to effectively communicate and collaborate with cross-functional teams and stakeholders. Part of effectively communicating is not to speak the language of quality but the language of the individuals you are trying to persuade.

- Ability to Benchmark: Knowledge of quality systems in other industries and drug development processes will be a big plus.
- Other Skills: Strong project management, analytical, and, most importantly, problem-solving skills.

Each year, I teach a class at my alma mater, Temple University School of Pharmacy, on Pharmaceutical Economics. The following are the first few slides I used in the class:

Shortly after Serving Patients is a Privilege Slides:

Over time, I met and became friends with these two incredible women. I consider Katherine Eban and Rosemary Gibson heroes. I highly recommend their books as excellent reading to understand where your medicines come from and the hidden risks you unknowingly take with some of your medications.

Chapter 3 - My Purpose

Do What is in the Best Interest of Patients:

What does "do what is in the best interest of patients" mean?

Simply put, patients need quality drugs that are affordable and available when patients need them.

As a trained pharmacist, I was taught to do what was in the best interest of patients and took an oath upon graduation to do just that. So, it makes sense that I would lead by example to do what is in the best interest of patients.

Most of the decisions I faced, living up to this mantra, were easy to implement and communicate with the larger team. However, in certain situations, these decisions are difficult to determine what is in the best interest of patients.

Chapter 4: Oath of a Pharmacist

Oath of a Pharmacist

I promise to devote myself to a lifetime of service to others through the profession of pharmacy. In fulfilling this vow:

I will consider the welfare of humanity and relief of suffering my primary concerns.

I will apply my knowledge, experience, and skills to the best of my ability to assure optimal outcomes for my patients.

I will respect and protect all personal and health information entrusted to me.

I will accept the lifelong obligation to improve my professional knowledge and competence.

I will hold myself and my colleagues to the highest principles of our profession's moral, ethical and legal conduct.

I will embrace and advocate changes that improve patient care.

I will utilize my knowledge, skills, experiences, and values to prepare the next generation of pharmacists.

I take these vows voluntarily with the full realization of the responsibility with which I am entrusted by the public.

American Association of
Colleges of Pharmacy **AACP**

Chapter 5 - How Did I Get Here

I was raised in a family with blue-collar roots. While my mother had a nursing degree from Germany, she chose to be a stay-at-home mom after immigrating to the United States as a governess for a Swiss family. On the other hand, my father was an International Brotherhood of Electrical Workers Union construction electrician. As a child, I never entertained the idea of pursuing higher education; instead, I had aspirations of becoming a professional baseball player or following in my father's footsteps as an electrician. As I was getting close to graduating high school, the building industry took a negative turn, and half of the Union electricians in Philadelphia were out of work. My father saw no future for me as an electrician and insisted I attend college.

The 1977 building industry downturn was a significant economic event in the United States, which affected the construction industry and the broader economy. The downturn was characterized by a steep decline in construction activity, rising unemployment in the industry, and falling prices for construction materials and housing.

During that period, I held multiple roles at Wynnewood Pharmacy, serving as a delivery boy, soda jerk, and short-order cook at the soda fountain. Then, I caught the attention of an experienced pharmacist named Claude, who took me under his wing. Claude introduced me to the world of pharmacy and taught me the necessary skills to succeed in the field.

By Jane and Michael Stern
Published initially 1998 Gourmet Magazine

My goal was to obtain a pharmacy degree, acquire the necessary license, and establish an independent pharmacy. However, the pharmacy landscape underwent significant changes during the five years I spent pursuing my degree. Chain pharmacies began to replace independent ones rapidly, leaving me unsure about my career path.

One day, while attending class, an announcement was made regarding National Pharmaceutical Council summer internships in the pharmaceutical industry. Without delay, I applied for one of these internships and was fortunate to be selected for a summer internship at Abbott Laboratories in North Chicago, Illinois. I was assigned to the oral solid dosage form R&D organization, where I gained valuable experience.

Within the organization, there were seven pharmacy interns, including myself. Throughout the summer, we toured various company departments, allowing us to gain a comprehensive understanding of the industry. During one of these tours, I was introduced to Stan, the sterile injectable pilot plant manager. Stan took all of us under his wing, providing exposure to sterile injectables and encouraging us to explore the Chicagoland area and enjoy our time there.

During this twelve-week internship, I met my now-wife, Cynthia, a fellow pharmacy student at the University of Tennessee. Despite her initial disbelief when I proposed at the end of the internship, a week later, Cynthia called me and suggested dates for our wedding. As a result, we have been happily married for forty years as of July 23, 2023, and with three adult daughters.

In 1982, during the holiday season, I called Stan to wish him a happy Chanukah. During our conversation, he inquired about my plans after graduation. I mentioned that I would be searching for a job in the industry, and he quickly informed me of a job opening in the pilot plant. After several discussions and interviews, I was offered the job.

During my time at Abbott, I made many friends and colleagues. One day, I heard that a friend of mine, Jerry, was leaving the company. When I mentioned this to Stan, he clarified that Jerry was taking a promotion to lead the Quality Engineering Organization. Later that same day, Stan approached me and encouraged me to apply for Jerry's old job.

I went through the interview process, and Larry, the Director of Quality, offered me the position to lead the Product Complaint Department, which I accepted.

Although the Product Complaint job had its challenges, it provided me with a unique opportunity to gain experience in all areas of the company, including sales, marketing, manufacturing, quality, regulatory, medical, and more. This advice led me to follow Jerry to lead the Quality Engineering department and pursue roles in plant management, overseeing the Quality Unit of multiple plants and eventually becoming the VP of Quality for the two billion dollar Hospital Products Division.

Through these experiences, I qualified for a turnaround opportunity at Bayer Healthcare, where I led the global biologics Quality Unit. This role led to my role as Senior Vice President and Chief Quality Officer at Amgen, where I spent ten years before deciding to retire and move to Florida.

Unexpectedly, in retirement, Dan Liljenquist called me with an idea about starting a non-profit pharmaceutical company, now known as Civica Rx.

My life and career have been shaped by hard work, determination, serendipity, and risk-taking.

Chapter 6 – Protecting Patients

As a quality professional in the pharmaceutical industry, protecting patients should always be your top priority. This responsibility means ensuring all processes and procedures are designed to provide safe and effective drugs.

The key to success is to make it easy for individuals to comply with the requirements. For example, requiring running through the gauntlet of bureaucracy makes it hard to comply and encourages individuals to develop workarounds.

When things go sideways, tough decisions are occasionally required, which require courage and conviction to do the right thing. However, doing the right thing to protect patients can be complex, especially when it conflicts with your employer's or colleagues' interests.

Sometimes, a quality professional may have to make the hardest decision – to protect patients at all costs, even if it means putting their job on the line. This approach can also be complex, requiring a willingness to stand up for what is right, even if it means going against the status quo or challenging established practices.

Putting patients first, even if it means risking your career, requires a solid moral compass and a commitment to ethical principles. Quality professionals must always strive to maintain the highest standards of integrity and honesty and be willing to speak out when they see something that could potentially harm patients.

A friend wanted to initiate a recall for a patient safety concern. However, as he began to socialize the issues within the company, his supervisor, the Head of Operations, would not support his decision and would not allow the recall. He then escalated the need for a drug recall to the CEO, who also would not allow the drug to be recalled. Within a few days, the Head of Quality was terminated.

Ultimately, the role of a quality professional is to serve as a patient advocate, ensuring that the care provided is of the highest quality and safety. Filling these duties requires a deep understanding of the complex systems and processes involved in drug development, manufacturing, and distribution and a commitment to ongoing education and learning. By always putting patients first, even in the face of tough decisions, quality professionals can help to create a safer and more effective healthcare system for everyone.

An Example Of A Quality Professional Failure

Intas Pharmaceuticals Limited

Intas faced severe scrutiny from the FDA in 2022 due to multiple issues described in a 36-page FDA Form 483. During their investigation, the FDA uncovered various problems, including lapses in record-keeping, poorly defined procedures and controls, and concerns about microbial contamination risk and environmental monitoring.

Most concerning were data integrity issues related to destroying numerous GMP records while the FDA was on site. Here is a quote from the FDA Form 483:

"Trash truck containing GMP documents mixed with general scrap: On 22-Nov-2022, we observed hundreds of transparent and black plastic bags containing torn pieces of analytical balance weight slips (printouts)....:"

The FDA discovered that Intas had incomplete lab records and inadequate procedures, such as inaccurate counting of environmental monitoring samples and a lack of a procedure for integrating hand-entered events. However, the most significant problem was found in Intas' quality control unit, where a lack of oversight on critical production documents led to a "cascade of failure."

During the inspection, FDA investigators noticed Intas employees from the quality control lab, production department, and engineering department destroying important documents related to original records and raw data. These documents were torn into pieces and discarded in Intas' quality control lab and parenteral scrap areas.

The FDA emphasized that these areas were crucial for manufacturing and testing Intas' medicines sold in the United States.

Intas' attempts to obscure the situation continued when FDA investigators found a truck filled with transparent plastic bags containing shredded documents and black plastic bags containing randomly torn documents mixed with other scrap materials. On the same day, investigators discovered more document scraps inside a large black plastic bag hidden under a staircase.

The records inside were wet, emitting a strong chemical smell. According to a general manager, the wet documents resulted from an acid spill that was cleaned using tissue papers, which were then discarded with other waste.

However, a quality control officer provided a different account, alleging that another employee immediately rushed to tear apart balance printouts and Auto Titrator spectrums upon learning of the investigators' arrival. The torn pieces were thrown into a small trash container and then treated with an acid solution to destroy potential evidence of tests with potentially damaging results.

The FDA also identified other problems, including inadequate procedures to prevent microbial contamination of sterile drugs, poorly monitored aseptic processing areas, insufficient process validation and stability testing, failure to investigate failures or deviations adequately, and unsecured computers and software.

In its final observation, the FDA criticized Intas for failing to establish its testing methods' accuracy, sensitivity, specificity, and reproducibility.

The FDA's findings revealed significant deficiencies in Intas' record-keeping, procedures, controls, and overall quality control practices.

An Example of the Right Quality Behavior:

McNeil Consumer Healthcare

Here is an example of where a Quality Professional did the right thing. McNeil Consumer Healthcare: In 2010, McNeil Consumer Healthcare promptly recalled over 40 different products, including Tylenol and Benadryl, due to manufacturing issues at their plants in Puerto Rico and Pennsylvania. The recalls were related to problems with quality control and contamination.

I confirmed one day that I was working for a great company when I had to notify the CEO and his staff during a meeting that we needed to initiate a significant recall. The CEO stressed that I "do the right thing" and that the entire company was at my disposal to do what was necessary to successfully implement the recall and figure out what went wrong and how to prevent the issue from happening again. Then, an hour later, the CEO came to my office to stress that I did the right thing, and he supported my decision 100%. He subsequently solidified his support through his actions, supplying resources and funds to implement the recall and address the root causes of the failures.

Chapter 7 - Quality from Medieval to Modern Times

The concept of quality has evolved through the ages, from the medieval guilds of master craftsmen to modern-day standards organizations. The history of quality is a long and complex one that the needs and demands of different societies and industries have shaped. I will explore the evolution of quality from the medieval guilds of master craftsmen to the present day.

At each progressive step, things improved. However, we should not forget that good practices and techniques exist at each stage of history. After a contractor completes a job, I often think, "I wish a craftsman completed that job." A craftsman is someone skilled in a particular craft or trade who uses their expertise to create or repair things by hand. They often spend years honing their skills through apprenticeships or formal training, and they may specialize in a particular type of craft or work across multiple fields. Nevertheless, they take pride in their workmanship and will not tolerate substandard work.

Starting in the Middle Ages, the guilds of master craftsmen were the primary guardians of quality. These guilds were made up of skilled artisans who produced goods of high quality, which were then sold to the public. Guild members were required to complete a rigorous apprenticeship and were subject to strict quality standards. These standards were enforced through regular inspections and testing, and any member who failed to meet the standards could be expelled from the guild.

We must learn from past developments and quality legends to instill a culture of quality and build a robust and consistent quality system, thus achieving a high level of performance.

During The Industrial Revolution

Mass production became the norm, and the role of the guilds in quality control began to decline. The focus shifted from individual craftsmanship to producing massive quantities of goods. Mass production methods were developed during the Industrial Revolution, but quality control was still focused on inspecting finished products. This approach was time-consuming and costly, as defective products had to be identified and removed from production. These problems led to a decrease in quality, as factories began to produce goods that were often poorly made and unreliable.

Quality control was introduced in the early 20th century, primarily in the United States. The development of statistical methods for quality control, such as the work of Walter Shewhart and W. Edwards Deming, led to the establishment of a formal quality control system. This system emphasized the importance of statistical process control and the need for continuous improvement in the production process.

Henry Ford's Contributions

"Quality means doing it right when no one is looking."

- Henry Ford

The concept of quality control was reintroduced in the United States with the contributions of Henry Ford. Ford is famous for introducing the assembly line, revolutionizing manufacturing, and making mass production possible. His focus on efficiency and standardization also led to significant improvements in quality control.

Ford recognized that each worker on the assembly line had a specific task and that any variation in that task could lead to defects in the final product. To address this issue, he developed the concept of interchangeable parts and implemented strict quality standards for each component. He also introduced statistical process control techniques to monitor and improve the production process.

Ford's contributions to quality control were significant, and his ideas were widely adopted in other industries. His efforts led to the development of formal quality control systems and helped to establish quality as a factor for a successful organization. Today, Ford's legacy lives on, and his contributions to quality control continue to influence modern manufacturing practices.

Henry Ford's quote, "Quality means doing it right when no one is looking," demonstrates the importance of establishing a quality culture.

Bell Telephone

In addition to Henry Ford's contributions, Bell Telephone's work in the early 20th century also helped advance the quality control concept. Bell Telephone pioneered the telecommunications industry and recognized the importance of quality in delivering reliable phone service to its customers.

One of Bell Telephone's most significant contributions was developing the concept of total quality control. This approach focused on involving all employees in the quality control process, from design to manufacturing to customer service. It also emphasized the importance of continuous improvement and the need to address quality issues at every stage of the production process.

Walter Stewhart was a Bell Telephone employee engineer who applied statistical methods and, in 1924, developed the control chart. He and his colleagues at Bell Telephone developed statistical quality control techniques that are still used today, such as control charts and sampling methods. These techniques helped to identify defects and improve the overall quality of their products.

The company's commitment to quality was reflected in its slogan, "One Policy, One System, Universal Service." This slogan reflected their belief that a universal commitment to quality was essential to providing reliable phone service to everyone.

Bell Telephone's contributions to quality control were significant, and their work helped to establish the importance of quality as a core business value. In addition, their focus on total quality control and continuous improvement paved the way for the development of modern quality management systems. Today, the principles of Total Quality Control, which led to Total Quality Management, are still used in industries worldwide, and Bell Telephone's legacy continues to influence how we think about quality.

World War II

WWII was a time of significant advances in quality control. The war effort required the production of massive quantities of goods, from weapons to food, and maintaining quality was critical to the success of the Allied forces. As a result, quality control became a strategic priority for governments and industries alike.

One of the most significant contributions to quality control during WWII was the development of statistical quality control techniques by W. Edwards Deming. Deming's work was instrumental in improving the quality of American military production, and his ideas would later be widely adopted by industry worldwide.

Deming's approach emphasized using statistical methods to measure and improve the quality of production processes. He also stressed the importance of involving all employees in the quality control process and using quality as a strategic tool to enhance overall business performance.

The Toyota Production System

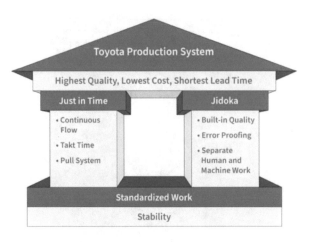

Toyota Production System (TPS) is a manufacturing system developed by Toyota in the 1950s. The system is based on continuous improvement, also known as kaizen, and is designed to eliminate waste and increase efficiency in manufacturing processes. The TPS has significantly impacted quality control and has been widely adopted by industries worldwide.

One of the critical features of the TPS is the focus on reducing waste, which is achieved by implementing the "just-in-time" inventory system. This system ensures that materials and parts are delivered to the production line exactly when needed, eliminating excess inventory and reducing the risk of defects caused by damaged or outdated components. By reducing waste and ensuring that only high-quality parts are used in production, the TPS has helped to improve the overall quality of Toyota's products.

Another aspect of the TPS is the emphasis on continuous improvement. This focus involves constantly evaluating and refining the production process to eliminate waste and improve efficiency. In addition, by encouraging employees to identify and address quality issues, TPS has helped foster a "culture of quality" within Toyota and has focused on producing high-quality products.

The TPS also places a strong emphasis on teamwork and employee involvement. This approach encourages employees to take ownership of their work and to work together to identify and solve quality problems. By involving employees in the quality control process, the TPS has helped foster a sense of pride and ownership in the quality of Toyota's products.

Overall, the Toyota Production System has significantly impacted quality control in the manufacturing industry. By reducing waste, promoting continuous improvement, and emphasizing employee involvement, the TPS has helped improve the overall quality of Toyota's products and has set a new standard for quality in the industry. As a result, other companies and industries have widely adopted the TPS principles and helped establish quality as a core business value.

Those individuals who have read my writings, heard me speak, or know me will wonder why I mention just-in-time inventory positively since I advocate for risk mitigation using inventories to ensure critical drugs are available when the patient needs to be treated.

As a quality professional, I support the steps required to implement just-in-time inventories effectively. However, I have not seen many in the pharmaceutical industry take the time to do the homework before implementing just-in-time inventories to reduce their costs.

Therefore, as a patient advocate, I must insist on keeping safety stock of raw materials and finished products to guarantee that patients can access insulin, cancer drugs, antibiotics, and many more medications.

Motorola

The war effort also led to developing other quality management techniques, such as Six Sigma, which Motorola used to improve the quality of its products during the war. Six Sigma is a statistical approach to quality control that focuses on identifying and eliminating defects in a process.

The war effort also led to the development of formal quality management systems, such as the ISO 9001 standard, first published in 1987. This standard provides a framework for implementing quality management systems and has become the most widely used standard worldwide.

Today, quality is a critical factor in the success of any organization. Customers demand high-quality goods and services, and companies that fail to deliver can quickly lose market share. As a result, quality standards are firmly entrenched in every industry, from manufacturing to healthcare to education. Quality management systems ensure that processes are efficient and effective and that products and services meet customers' needs.

In conclusion, the concept of quality has evolved significantly over time, from the strict quality control of the medieval guilds of master craftsmen to the modern-day quality management systems used by organizations worldwide. The history of quality is a story of continuous improvement driven by consumer needs and demands, technological advances, and global marketplace changes. The evolution of quality has led to a world where high-quality goods and services are expected, and organizations that fail to deliver can quickly fall behind their competitors.

Chapter 8 - The Legends of Quality

There have been many legendary quality leaders throughout history. Here are a few notable ones. However, not one legendary quality leader worked full-time within the pharmaceutical industry.

Therefore, I studied the following individuals' approaches and theories and used that information to develop strategies for leading various pharma quality organizations.

Will you be the first legendary quality leader in pharma, and what will you need to become that legendary quality leader?

W. Edwards Deming (1900-1993)

W. Edwards Deming was an American statistician, engineer, and management consultant considered the father of the quality movement. He believed that by improving processes and systems, companies could achieve higher levels of quality and productivity. Deming's philosophy emphasized that quality was everyone's responsibility and that involving all employees in continuous improvement would create a "culture of quality" to drive innovation and growth.

His teachings significantly impacted Japan's manufacturing industry in the 1950s and 1960s and gradually gained acceptance in the United States.

His famous "14 Points for Management" provided a framework for implementing a quality management system. In addition, his emphasis on the importance of statistical analysis and continuous improvement continues to be a key component of quality management practices today.

Taiichi Ohno (1912-1990)

Taiichi Ohno was a Japanese industrial engineer and businessman best known for developing the Toyota Production System or Lean Manufacturing. Ohno believed the key to improving manufacturing efficiency was eliminating waste, or "muda," from the production process. Muda is a Japanese term that refers to any activity or process that does not add value or contribute to producing a product or service.

Eliminating muda is a crucial principle of lean manufacturing, and lean practitioners focus on identifying and eliminating waste in all aspects of the production process. Ohno's Toyota Production System was built around several core principles, including just-in-time production and "jidoka," which involved building quality control at every step of the production process to ensure defects were caught and corrected as early as possible.

Jidoka is a Japanese term used in lean manufacturing and refers to the concept of "automation with a human touch." Ohno was also known for his emphasis on continuous improvement, or "kaizen," which involved constantly looking to improve processes and eliminate waste.

Shigeo Shingo (1909 – 1990)

Shigeo Shingo was a Japanese industrial engineer and manufacturing consultant known for his work on the Toyota Production System. He developed several industrial engineering practices, including the Single-Minute Exchange of Die (SMED) system.

SMED is a technique that reduces the time required to change a production line from one product to another.

Shingo's work on the Toyota Production System focused on identifying and eliminating waste in the production process. He is considered a key figure in the development of lean manufacturing practices. He emphasized the importance of focusing on the entire production process, from supplier to customer and developing a deep understanding of every aspect of the process to identify improvement opportunities.

Joseph Juran (1904 – 2008)

Joseph Juran was a management consultant and engineer who made significant contributions to the field of quality management. He developed the Quality Trilogy, which consists of three interrelated processes: quality planning, quality control, and quality improvement.

He emphasized the importance of quality in all aspects of an organization's operations. He promoted the idea of a quality culture where all employees are committed to achieving high levels of quality in their work. Juran also pioneered using statistical methods in quality management and developed several statistical tools and techniques for quality improvement.

Armand Feigenbaum (1920 – 2014)

Armand Feigenbaum was an American quality control expert and management consultant who founded General Systems Company, a management consulting firm specializing in quality control and productivity improvement. He is best known for his work on total quality control (TQC), which emphasizes the importance of quality throughout the organization. Feigenbaum believed that TQC was essential for achieving and maintaining a competitive advantage in today's global marketplace.

He developed the concept of the "hidden plant," which refers to the resources and potential productivity wasted in a poorly organized and managed system. Feigenbaum's ideas and principles continue to influence quality management practices worldwide, and his legacy lives on through the continued use of TQC methodologies in many industries and organizations.

Philip Crosby (1926 – 2001)

Philip Crosby was an American quality management expert and author who developed the concept of "zero defects," emphasizing the importance of preventing defects rather than correcting them. Crosby believed that quality should be an essential part of an organization's culture and that everyone should be committed to achieving zero defects. He developed a four-step quality improvement process and strongly advocated using statistical process control (SPC) in quality management.

Crosby's ideas and principles continue to influence quality management practices worldwide.

Kaoru Ishikawa (1915 – 1989)

Kaoru Ishikawa was a Japanese engineer and quality management expert who made significant contributions to the field of quality management. He believed identifying and addressing quality problems systematically and in a data-driven way was essential.

He is best known for his work on developing and applying statistical process control (SPC) and quality control tools. Ishikawa developed several quality control tools, including the Ishikawa diagram and the Pareto chart, which identify and analyze the causes of a particular problem or quality issue and prioritize and focus on the most significant reasons. He also emphasized the importance of employee involvement in quality management and promoted the idea of quality circles, where groups of employees meet regularly to identify and solve quality problems. Ishikawa published several influential books on quality management, and his concepts and principles continue to influence quality management practices today.

What About Pharma:
Who is the Legendary Quality Leader

I must admit that many pharmaceutical companies have not embraced many of the principles proven to work by other industries as taught by Historical Quality Leaders. Many generic drug companies believe these principles are too expensive and cannot afford to implement these measures. As an individual who has spoken at many conferences about quality, I am inevitably asked during the question and answer section, "How do I convince my management to spend the money to do the right thing?" or something similar to this question.

However, it is not entirely accurate to say that the pharmaceutical industry has not embraced quality principles. The fact is that the pharmaceutical industry has a long history of producing drugs to quality standards and regulations. However, this is accomplished using testing and inspecting approaches. A mentor and friend once said, "Our manufacturing practices perform at 3 Sigma, but the product delivered to patients meets 6 Sigma requirements." Of course, the FDA will say that you can't test and inspect the quality of the product; it has to be designed and built into the product. However, international laws, regulations, and government guidances actually promote a testing and inspecting approach to ensure drug quality.

Here is just one example where the pharmaceutical industry tests and inspects the quality of its products versus building in quality.

A McKinsey POBOS database with 27,000 pieces of equipment data indicates:

- There are 100 to 300 hours of unplanned downtime per line (approximately a 10% OEE loss due to container handling failures.
- Equipment running at 75% rated speed due to container damage and flow optimization concerns.
- Greater than 10% of changeovers require rework due to improper set-up.

McKinsey data demonstrates that $10 Million can be saved annually per manufacturing line by addressing glass handling issues.

This example demonstrates why quality is free.

Every glass container is 100% visually inspected to ensure that glass defects do not escape the manufacturing facility and make their way to the patient.

The industry is heavily regulated by government agencies, such as the US Food and Drug Administration (FDA) and the European Medicines Agency (EMA), which require companies to comply with strict quality standards to ensure the safety and efficacy of their products.

Additionally, the pharmaceutical industry has developed quality management systems, such as Good Manufacturing Practices (GMP), Good Laboratory Practices (GLP), and Good Distributions Practices (GDP), designed to ensure that products are manufactured and tested according to established standards and procedures.

However, the pharmaceutical sector is not immune to quality issues, and there have been cases where companies have fallen short of the expected high standards. In these instances, the industry needs to learn from its mistakes and continuously improve its quality management systems.

It is essential to expel unethical players from the pharmaceutical ecosystem. Recently, the FDA inspected an Intas site in December 2022, and the FDA found too many incidents of data integrity events to count, including the destruction of raw data, during the inspection. If proven accurate, the entire Intas leadership team should be banned (disbarred) from ever selling drugs within the United States. The FDA 36-page Form 483 is available online from the FDA.

There is a race to get to the market fast in the pharmaceutical industry for both brand and generic drugs. Part of the justification to get to the market fast is altruistic to help treat patients or to save patients money. However, there is also a profit motive. The sooner a branded drug enters the market, the more revenue is generated. The first company to file its application with the FDA for a generic drug approval acquires 180 days of market exclusivity in the United States, decreasing competition and keeping prices high.

Chapter 9 - My Early Career

I was recently married, moved to a new state, and purchased our first home, having less than $500 in savings when the following events occurred.

One day, my boss was out of town, and I was placed in charge. A minor stray mark was detected on the label during a line setup. I decided entirely on instinct to continue running the line since I was not aware of the work done by the Legends of Quality.

The line ran faster than it had ever run before, which was the cause of the minor defect.

A few weeks later, the customer detected a minor defect and would not accept the batch and rejected the product. My boss called me into the office and said the customer rejected around $1 million of product because of the label defect and asked what happened.

At that point, I was convinced I would lose my job. So, I began to explain what happened, what was discovered, and that I felt the defect was minor and insignificant.

I then asked, with a crackling voice, if I was going to get fired.

My boss leaned back in his chair and said, "Fire you? I just spent $1 Million training you."

At that point, he gave me the first book on Quality that I had ever read.

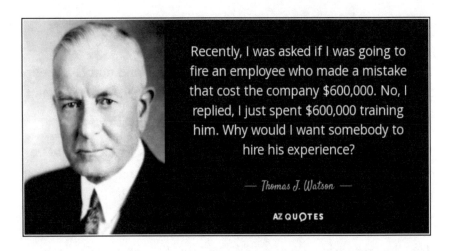

Recently, I was asked if I was going to fire an employee who made a mistake that cost the company $600,000. No, I replied, I just spent $600,000 training him. Why would I want somebody to hire his experience?

— Thomas J. Watson —

AZ QUOTES

I have also used this quote several times with various staff members throughout my career.

Chapter 10 - Do What is in the Best Interest of Patients

What does "do what is in the best interest of patients" mean?

Simply put, patients need quality drugs that are affordable and available when patients need them. This mantra is simple to say but hard to achieve. To succeed, one must fulfill all three of these attributes, or one will fail to do what is in the best interest of patients.

When I co-founded Civica Rx, on day one, this became our mantra which drives Civica leaders and employees. The address for the Civica manufacturing facility is One Civica Way. Because there is only one way to do things at Civica: **"The Right Way!"**

William and Charles Mayo, MDs >>

"The Best interest of the patient is the only interest to be considered."

As a trained pharmacist, I was taught to do what was in the best interest of patients and took an oath upon graduation to do just that. So, it makes sense that I would lead by example to do what is in the best interest of patients. Most of the decisions I faced, living up to this mantra, are easy to implement and communicate with the larger team. However, in certain situations, determining what is in the best interest of patients is complex.

The most challenging part of living up to the mantra "Do what is in the best interest of patients; that is what we will do" is balancing multiple stakeholders' needs and interests while maintaining the organization's viability. While the main focus of the mantra is on serving patients' needs, many other stakeholders are involved in the healthcare ecosystem, such as providers, payers, regulators, and shareholders. At the end of the day, you need to serve patients while at the same time remaining a viable entity to continue to meet patient needs.

A simple example would be that it benefits patients for drugs to be inexpensive. However, some say providing the drug for free is in the best interest of patients. But would that really help patients if the provider cuts corners, produces substandard quality drugs, runs afoul of the regulators, becomes financially unsustainable, and goes out of business? Then, other competitors could significantly raise the price, or the drug is no longer available. I can imagine many similar situations where the solutions would look like they were in the best interest of patients, but, in reality, the decisions actually harm patients.

Here is a recent example of policies mandated, with good intentions, by a national opioid settlement designed to respond to the opioid addiction and overdose crisis by limiting the quantity of opioids produced and distributed. Unfortunately, this policy created an unintended consequence, making filling legitimate prescriptions for Attention Deficit Hyperactivity Disorder, Narcolepsy, and Anxiety a significant headache. (Described in Ike Swetliz's article "Xanax and Adderall Access Is Being Blocked by Secret Drug Limits" Bloomberg News – April 3, 2023)

The most challenging part of Doing What is in the Best Interest of Patients in these situations is developing effective communications to prove the approach is the correct approach. The key in these cases is to have a communication plan with the impacted stakeholders that clearly defines the reason for the decision, the options considered, and the conclusion of why the decision was in the best interest of patients.

A Funny but True Personal Story About Doing What is in the Best Interest of Patients.

Once upon a time, I was a director of quality overseeing several plants. One of the plants kept having failures, and after some investigation, we discovered that the laboratory was to blame. But we couldn't determine why the laboratory had such difficulty getting it right.

I knew this would be a controversial conclusion, so we had to run several experiments using several laboratories. These experiments proved that the failures were a result of laboratory error. Unfortunately, the investigation and experiments took time, and approved inventories were tight. Then, we still could not figure out why the laboratory was having difficulties.

Now, I had to deal with the actual probability of numerous drug shortages. That is when I decided to have one of the other laboratories conduct the release testing to ensure that there would not be any drug shortages.

The next problem was the availability of samples from the batches' beginning, middle, and end as required per our procedures and approved regulatory applications. This problem existed because the order of filled and packaged vials was not maintained throughout the manufacturing process, and we had limited samples pulled contemporaneously for each sample set.

I did not want to take the chance of losing the samples or damaging them via shipping with UPS or FedEx.

So, I came up with a crazy plan. First, I purchased a round-trip airline ticket to one of the other cities where the laboratory successfully conducted the testing. Then, I arranged for the Head of Quality of that site to meet me at the airport, accept the samples, and begin testing the various products.

But, of course, the return flight was on the same plane and with the same aircrew; I even had the same seat assignment for both flights. You may ask why I did that, and I would say, because why not?

After transferring the samples, I purchased a hot dog and a soft drink before boarding the plane.

Once I was seated and the flight attendant walked through the aisle, she stopped, looked at me with her head tilted to one side, and asked, "Did I see you on the inbound flight?" I responded that she did see me on that flight. She then asked, "Why?" I replied that this airport had the best hot dogs in the world, and I wanted a hot dog. She was amazed at my response. Then, I told her what had happened, and we both had a good laugh.

Then, at the next FDA GMP Inspection, the FDA Investigator wanted to review the situation. The FDA Investigator asked if the laboratory that successfully completed the testing was listed in the Abbreviated New Drug Applications for those drugs. The laboratory was FDA approved but not for those drugs, which was the hard decision that had to be made to prevent drug shortages. A lengthy discussion occurred that included individuals from FDA Headquarters. Eventually, the FDA concluded that we did the right thing and just wished we had given them a heads-up. Long after these events, after I retired, I asked an individual from the FDA who was knowledgeable about these events one question. Would the FDA have allowed me to act quickly to prevent potential drug shortages? The individuals did not even take a moment to consider the response and responded, "No Way."

To be a successful quality executive, you often have confusing and incomplete data, making a decision hard. However, you must find a solution that maintains quality and compliance while ensuring patients can be treated when the drug is needed. That means that sometimes you need to be creative, think out of the box, and take calculated chances based on the data you have.

Chapter 11 -What I Think Quality Means

Quality means meeting or exceeding the customer's expectations. Since the industry has several stakeholders, from consumers, patients, healthcare providers, healthcare systems, and even the FDA, delighting all these customers is challenging. However, a good start is ensuring the medications are safe, effective, consistent, reliable, of good quality, available, and affordable (value).

Safe and Effective

Patients and healthcare providers expect that companies' drugs are safe and effective for their intended use. They want to be sure that the products will produce the desired results and not cause any harm.

Consistent and Reliable

A consistent and reliable drug consistently produces the desired therapeutic effect and does so reliably over time.

Consistency refers to the drug's ability to produce the same effects every time it is used, regardless of the batch or manufacturing process. A consistent drug has a uniform composition and potency, which ensures that patients receive the correct dosage and that the drug is effective.

Reliability refers to the drug's ability to consistently produce the desired therapeutic effect over time. A reliable drug always has the same therapeutic effect with each use and does not produce unexpected or harmful side effects.

In summary, a consistent and reliable drug is predictable in its effects. It is safe and effective in treating the condition it was designed for.

Quality

A quality drug is a drug that meets established standards for safety, purity, potency, and efficacy. In other words, it is a drug that is of high quality and has been manufactured and tested to ensure that it is safe and effective for its intended use.

Factors contributing to a drug's quality include its manufacturing process, composition, and packaging. For example, a drug manufactured using Good Manufacturing Practices (GMP) is more likely to be of high quality because GMP ensures that the drug is manufactured under strict quality control measures to minimize the risk of contamination or errors during production. Additionally, a drug that is appropriately labeled and packaged to protect it from light, moisture, and other environmental factors can help ensure that it remains stable and effective over time.

A quality drug has undergone rigorous testing and meets high safety, purity, potency, and efficacy standards. In addition, it is manufactured and packaged to maintain its quality throughout its shelf life.

Availability

Drug availability refers to the ability of patients to access a particular drug. This access can include factors such as the drug's availability in local pharmacies or healthcare facilities, its cost, and any regulatory restrictions on its use.

The availability of a drug can be influenced by numerous factors, including its manufacturing and distribution, government regulations, and market demand. For example, some medications may not be available in certain countries due to regulatory restrictions, in short supply, or only through prescription from a healthcare provider.

Some patients may also face barriers to accessing drugs due to the limited availability of healthcare facilities or other logistical challenges.

Drug availability is essential to ensuring access to healthcare for all patients. Governments, healthcare providers, and drug manufacturers can work together to improve drug availability by improving distribution networks, increasing funding for healthcare programs, and reducing regulatory barriers to drug access.

Lack of product availability can significantly impact patients' health and well-being. It can lead to delays in treatment, increased healthcare costs, and even cause harm if a patient cannot access a necessary medication.

Affordability or Value

The affordability or value of a drug refers to its cost versus the benefits it provides to patients. In other words, it measures how much patients are willing to pay for the drug relative to its therapeutic value.

The affordability of a drug can be influenced by numerous factors, including its manufacturing cost, research and development costs, marketing costs, and government regulations. Additionally, the availability of generic drug versions can impact its affordability, as generic drugs tend to be less expensive than brand-name drugs.

On the other hand, the value of a drug is determined by its clinical benefits, such as its effectiveness in treating a particular condition, its safety profile, and its impact on patient outcomes. A drug that provides significant clinical benefits and improves patient outcomes is highly valued.

Overall, the affordability and value of a drug are essential considerations in healthcare decision-making. Policymakers, healthcare providers, and patients must balance the costs of drugs with their clinical benefits to ensure patients have access to affordable treatments that provide the most significant value.

Chapter 12 - Quality Matters

Why Must Quality Professionals Promote Quality Across Their Organizations?

Pharmaceutical quality professionals play a crucial role in ensuring that their companies' medicines and healthcare products are safe, effective, consistent, and reliable. However, the importance of quality may not always be fully appreciated or understood by other departments within the company. Obtaining voluntary actions is much more effective than issuing dictates; however, quality dictates are sometimes necessary.

There are several reasons why pharmaceutical quality professionals must learn to promote the importance of quality within their companies.

The most effective Quality Heads must be the Quality Chief Sales and Marketing Officer!

Firstly, promoting the importance of quality helps create a "culture of quality" throughout the organization. When quality is understood and valued across all departments, it becomes a shared responsibility, not just the quality department's responsibility. This shared responsibility can lead to better quality outcomes, increased productivity, and improved customer satisfaction.

Secondly, promoting the importance of quality can help to ensure compliance with regulations and standards. Regulations and quality standards are constantly evolving, and the quality department's responsibility is to ensure that the company remains compliant. When other departments understand the importance of quality, they are more likely to comply with regulations and standards, reducing the risk of regulatory action and reputational damage.

Thirdly, promoting the importance of quality can help identify and mitigate risks. Quality professionals are trained to identify and mitigate risks throughout product development and manufacturing. When other departments understand the importance of quality, they are more likely to identify and report potential risks, allowing the quality department to take appropriate action.

Overall, promoting quality within a pharmaceutical company ensures that products are safe, effective, consistent, and reliable. It also helps to create a quality culture, ensure compliance with regulations and standards, and identify and mitigate risks.

The Quality organization must address a significant quality issue immediately to ensure patient safety, product quality, or regulatory compliance. A quality dictate is a directive or order issued by the quality department to halt production, recall products, or take other actions to address a quality issue.

There are several situations in which quality dictates may be necessary:

Quality dictates may be required when an identified serious quality issue poses a risk to patient safety or product quality. These dictates could include contamination, impurities, or packaging defects.

Quality dictates may be necessary when the company violates regulations or standards. These violations could include failure to follow Good Manufacturing Practices (GMP).

Quality dictates may be necessary when initiating a product recall. For example, product recalls could include situations where a product is found to be defective or potentially harmful to patients.

Quality dictates may be necessary when a change in regulations or standards affects the company's operations. For example, these regulations could include changes in labeling requirements, product testing, or manufacturing practices.

In all these situations, quality dictates are necessary to ensure quality issues are dealt with promptly and effectively. The goal is to protect patient safety, maintain product quality, and ensure compliance with regulations and standards.

Pharmaceutical quality professionals need to learn how to promote the importance of quality within their companies without dictates. Here are some strategies that can be effective:

- Quality professionals can work with their colleagues in marketing or communications to develop a comprehensive communication strategy that effectively promotes the importance of quality within the company. These communications can include internal newsletters, regular training sessions, and presentations to different departments.
- Quality professionals should build relationships with other departments and stakeholders within the company to understand their priorities and concerns. By doing so, they can tailor their message and communicate the importance of quality in a way that resonates with each department.
- Quality professionals can use data to demonstrate the value of quality to other departments. These data types include customer satisfaction, regulatory compliance, and product quality data. By showing the impact of quality on the company's bottom line, quality professionals can help to build support for quality across the organization.
- Quality professionals should encourage collaboration across different departments and teams to ensure that quality is a shared responsibility. These collaborations can include cross-functional teams, joint meetings, and sharing of best practices.

Finally, quality professionals should lead by example and demonstrate their commitment to quality in their day-to-day work. By showing the importance of quality in their work, they can inspire others to do the same and build a quality culture throughout the organization.

Promoting the importance of quality within a pharmaceutical company requires a comprehensive approach that involves effective communication, collaboration, and data-driven decision-making. By taking these steps, quality professionals can help ensure that products are safe, effective, consistent, and reliable while also building a "culture of quality" throughout the organization.

Chapter 13 - Where to Start

I must admit there is no single or perfect way to attack these tasks. But first, you should assess the completeness and effectiveness of the quality system, organization, and leadership across all functions. Then, from there, create a game plan. However, in my forty-year career, I have seen some trends. Look deeply for recurring situations that lead to quality and/or compliance troubles.

Is the quality organization respected and has power within the company? Here are some key indicators that there are problems or problems that will develop soon. For example, is the quality organization independent of manufacturing, or does it report to manufacturing? Can someone overturn a product rejection decision made at the plant level? Is quality thought of as compliance? How are supplies selected and monitored? Are processes out of control? Do analytical methods generate high invalid rates? How many human errors occur? Does it take a long time to release products? Does the organization look to the outside to benchmark and identify new quality tools, trends, or risks?

I will share some of my experiences, solutions, and funny stories in the upcoming chapters.

Chapter 14 - Building a "Culture of Quality"

Building a culture of quality requires a sustained effort involving every organization member. However, the CEO plays an essential role in shaping an organization's culture and building a quality culture. A quality culture requires the participation and commitment of every organization member, from the top down to the bottom up.

The CEO can set the tone for the organization by defining its vision, mission, and values and demonstrating a solid commitment to quality in everything they do. The CEO's actions and words set an example for others to follow.

They can help create a "culture of quality" by emphasizing the importance of quality, making it a priority, and rewarding those who contribute to it.

However, building a culture of quality is not solely the responsibility of the CEO. It requires the involvement of everyone in the organization, from the board of directors to the front-line employees. Every member of the organization has a role to play in building and sustaining a culture of quality. Everyone must be committed to prioritizing quality in all aspects of their work.

Here are some steps you can take to build a culture of quality:

- Define quality: Clearly define what quality means for your organization. This definition will help everyone understand what is expected of them and what they must do to achieve it.
- Communicate expectations: Communicate the quality expectations to everyone in the organization. Ensure everyone understands the importance of quality and how it contributes to the organization's success.
- Lead by example: Leaders play a critical role in building a culture of quality. They must lead by example and demonstrate a commitment to quality in everything they do.
- Provide training: Training helps employees understand what quality means, how to achieve it, and how to measure it. Ensure everyone has the knowledge and skills to contribute to the organization's quality goals.
- Foster teamwork: Quality is a team effort. Encourage teamwork and collaboration among employees to achieve quality goals. Reward teamwork and recognize individual contributions to the team's success.
- Continuously improve: Quality is not a one-time event. It is a continuous process of improvement. Encourage everyone to identify improvement areas and work together to implement solutions.
- Encourage an attitude to leave no stone unturned when investigating failures or making improvements.

- Measure and track progress: Measure and track progress toward quality goals. Use data to identify areas for improvement and to track progress over time. Use this information to make data-driven decisions and to continuously improve.
- Do not punish individuals who report or discover quality problems; praise them for their diligence.
- Suppose some individuals resist embracing quality within the organization by being passive-aggressive, consistently resisting change, or sabotaging the effort to create a quality culture. Identify them promptly, call them out, and deal with them swiftly. Do not ignore these behaviors from anyone. My biggest mistake in my career was allowing a long-term employee who would never change to hang around in their job for far too long.

By following these steps, you can build a culture of quality in your organization that will help drive success and continuous improvement. It also cements the reputation of and instills power within the quality organization.

Chapter 15 - Quality vs. Compliance

To be an effective quality professional, build an effective quality system, and create a "culture of quality," one must understand the difference between quality and compliance and where they overlap.

What is the difference between quality and compliance in the pharmaceutical industry? Quality and compliance are closely related concepts in the pharmaceutical industry but have different meanings and applications.

Quality refers to the degree to which a drug product meets its intended specifications and is safe, effective, and consistent. Quality is a core concern in the pharmaceutical industry. Companies must have robust quality management systems to ensure their products meet all relevant quality standards and regulations.

Conversely, compliance refers to the degree to which a company adheres to regulatory requirements and industry standards. Compliance is essential for ensuring that drugs are safe, effective, and meet regulatory requirements, and it is a critical part of maintaining quality in the pharmaceutical industry.

While quality and compliance are distinct concepts, they are linked. Quality is an essential component of compliance, and companies must demonstrate that their products meet all relevant quality standards and regulations to be compliant.

Overall, quality and compliance are both critical considerations in the pharmaceutical industry, and companies must prioritize both to ensure the safety and efficacy of their products.

Does compliance ensure quality?

Compliance is essential in the pharmaceutical industry, but it alone does not guarantee product quality.

While compliance is essential for ensuring that drugs meet regulatory requirements, it is only one aspect of quality management. Quality management also involves various activities, including developing and maintaining product knowledge; developing robust manufacturing processes; implementing the proper quality control procedures; and continuously monitoring and improving processes to ensure product quality.

Thus, while compliance is an essential component of quality management, it does not guarantee product quality. Therefore, companies must also prioritize other aspects of quality management to ensure that their products are safe, effective, and meet the intended specifications.

Does quality ensure compliance?

I believe and promote that having significant product knowledge, robust and repeatable manufacturing processes, well-designed control procedures, and continuously monitoring and improving the process will prevent non-conformances, defects, product failures, product complaints, and recalls. Thus, quality will ensure a significant level of compliance. Of course, that does not mean a regulatory observation will never be issued; however, I cannot see any significant observations if the quality system is driving the 6-Sigma product and process performance.

While quality is essential to regulatory compliance, it does not guarantee absolute compliance. Therefore, companies must prioritize quality and pay attention to compliance to ensure their products are safe, effective, and meet regulatory requirements.

On the other hand, being compliant does not guarantee quality.

In my opinion, too many companies don't see the difference and fail to invest appropriately in quality; thus, as a result, they are forced to spend too much on compliance.

Chapter 16 - Preventing Human Errors

One initiative you can work on to improve quality or go from "Good to Great" is preventing human errors.

Preventing human error is a complex and multifaceted issue. The act of retraining individuals, which is often used as a corrective action, is not effective.

Human Errors have to be engineered out of the process. Here are some strategies that may help reduce the likelihood of human error:

- Implement clear and concise standardized operating procedures and protocols for tasks that are performed regularly to help minimize the possibility of human error. Long, wordy Standard Operating Procedures are not effective. Instead, effective Standard Operating Procedures should use diagrams, photos, checklists, and videos to assist with complex tasks.

- Ensure that personnel are appropriately trained and knowledgeable about their tasks. Provide ongoing training to reinforce best practices and update skills. For effectiveness, use various training methods, such as classroom instruction, hands-on training, on-the-job training, simulations, and e-learning, to appeal to different learning styles and reinforce critical concepts. Finally, evaluate the effectiveness of the training program through assessments, tests, and employee feedback to identify areas where improvements can be made.

- Implement a Repeat Back Process for critical tasks that depend on humans for success. For example, this process can be used when regulations require documentation of who performed and verified the tasks.

- Consider automating tasks where possible to eliminate or reduce the possibility of human error. This automation can be done through the use of technology or machinery.

- Promote open communication channels to encourage the reporting of errors and near misses, which can help identify areas for improvement.
- Incorporate human factors engineering into the design of equipment, systems, and workspaces to make them more ergonomic and user-friendly.
- Foster a culture of continuous improvement and encourage feedback from personnel to identify areas for improvement and implement changes as necessary.

It is important to note that human error can never be entirely eliminated, but these strategies can help reduce the likelihood of errors and improve overall performance.

An effective SOP (Standard Operating Procedure)

An effective SOP is a document that outlines a clear and detailed set of instructions for completing a specific task or process. Here are some steps to help you write an effective SOP:

- Before you begin writing the SOP, you must determine the document's purpose and the process it will cover. Make sure you have a clear understanding of the task or process you are documenting.
- Determine whom the document is intended for and the level of detail they need. For example, suppose the procedure is for internal use. In that case, you may assume some knowledge about the process, while for external stakeholders, you may need to provide more background information.
- Create a detailed outline of the steps involved in the process, including any potential issues or challenges that may arise.
- Always keep in mind who is the SOP's audience. The author is rarely the audience. SOPs for operators, technicians, analysts, etc., should not be written for their supervisor, who probably sits in an office environment. The purpose of the SOP is to allow the individual performing the task to be successful.
- Use simple and plain language to ensure the target audience easily understands the SOP. Avoid using technical jargon or industry-specific terms that may be unfamiliar to the reader.

- Use diagrams, flowcharts, pictures, embedded videos, or other visual aids to help explain the process and make it easier to follow. It is said that a picture is worth a thousand words, and research demonstrates that a video is worth a million words. So why is there resistance to using videos embedded in SOPs? Just think how often individuals go to youtube to watch a how-to video to perform a task effectively, even though they have never performed that task.
- Provide clear, step-by-step instructions for completing each part of the process. Use bullet points, numbering, or other formatting techniques to make the instructions easy to follow.
- Write the SOP to make it easy for the impacted audience to be successful.
- Once you have completed the SOP, test it to ensure the SOP is accurate and the instructions are clear and easy to follow. Get feedback from other team members or stakeholders to ensure the document is effective.
- Make sure to update the SOP regularly to reflect any changes in the process or the latest information that may become available. Keep the document current and relevant to ensure the SOP continues to be effective.

In summary:

An SOP should be CLEAR AND CONCISE and not Stacks of Papers.

Write SOPs for the USER, and NOT THE AUTHOR

Embedding Video to Enhance SOPs

Say goodbye to dull, text-heavy SOPs...

The video has been adopted in some pharmaceutical Standard Operating Procedures (SOPs) as a complementary tool but is not widely used in the industry. I have heard various excuses for why they are not used.

The FDA will not accept this practice.

How do you validate the video?

It has never been done.

I bet you have heard of other excuses and myths which can be easily debunked.

A legitimate reason could be that an SOP often involves complex procedures and processes that may be difficult to capture on video. Filming every process step can be challenging, and the resulting video may be lengthy and difficult to navigate. Written procedures may be more concise and easier to follow.

Bite-size video clips can be a valuable tool in pharmaceutical SOPs for several reasons:

- Seeing is the best way to understand many of the physical tasks carried out in Pharma. A short, well-annotated video would trounce many of the SOPs I have read in terms of communicating the how.
- Videos can be used to demonstrate complex procedures or techniques that are difficult to describe in writing. Seeing the process in action can help employees better understand how to perform it correctly.

- Some individuals learn better through visual aids than through written instructions. Video can be a more engaging and effective way to communicate information for these learners.
- Video can help ensure consistency in procedures across various locations and employees. In addition, video can help reduce variation and ensure that all employees follow the same process by visually representing the correct procedure.
- Videos are handy to show how to conduct a rarely performed task that is not routine, such as performing preventative maintenance annually.
- Videos can be used to demonstrate safety procedures and highlight potential hazards. Employees can better understand how to stay safe on the job by visually representing the correct safety procedure. Think about your last flight on a commercial airliner.

Overall, video can be a valuable tool in pharmaceutical SOPs, particularly for demonstrating procedures, improving consistency, and enhancing employee learning and safety. Using video requires no additional controls other than a written SOP, and by effectively preventing errors, I cannot see why the FDA would not accept this practice.

For example, I tried to replace the brake light in my car. I could not figure out how to get to the light bulb to replace it. After 30 minutes of trying to get to the light bulb, I watched a YouTube video on how to perform this task. It is like a lightbulb going off in my head. The job became easier to complete, and in 5 minutes, I successfully replaced the light bulb.

Watching a short video is more effective and efficient than understanding and following a long, wordy SOP.

A previous colleague posted on LinkedIn the following:

"I was able to introduce the use of video to complete method transfers during the pandemic (using smart glasses). This was a great solution to be able to train QC analysts in real-time, with the added benefit that videos were saved, allowing analysts to review critical steps on demand. It took some convincing at first, as Martin Van Trieste mentions here, since this is not a conventional approach. However, a well-thought-out plan was all that was needed to implement. Too bad it took a global pandemic to convince leadership and stakeholders of the benefits of this technology.

I am so glad this was done, as it gave us the opportunity to actually improve the methods by watching execution on POV from the trainer's perspective and finding opportunities to improve consistency between analysts on assay execution. I'm glad he had the fortitude to drive forward and deliver a valuable tool for his QC analyst."

Repeat Back Process to Minimize Human Errors

I had the honor of spending time at sea on the USS Ronald Reagan (CVN 76), a nuclear aircraft carrier, and the USS Hampton (SSN-767), a nuclear attack submarine, to learn about the US Nuclear Navy Quality System and Risk Management process.

Photo: Taken by me on my voyage on the USS Hampton

The repeat-back process is a communication technique to ensure that the sender and receiver accurately transmit and understand information. Implementing this process was the most effective measure I ever implemented to prevent human errors.

This implementation alone reduced human errors by 90%. Here is how the repeat-back process works:

- The sender conveys a message or instruction to the receiver.
- The receiver repeats the message or instruction to the sender as a question.
- The sender listens carefully to confirm whether the message was repeated correctly or if any corrections are necessary. (This step is optional in some scenarios. However, I always recommend using this step)

The repeat back process is commonly used in high-risk industries such as aviation, healthcare, and nuclear power, where errors can have grave consequences. Here are some examples of when the repeat-back process may be used:

Photo: Taken by me on my voyage on the USS Ronald Reagan

Officer of the Deck (OOD): When the Officer of the Deck instructs the Helmsman to change course on a ship. Here's an example of a correct response that requires no further intervention by the OOD:

The officer issues an order: Helm, come right to course 1, 8, 0.
Helmsman Responds: Come right to course 1, 8, 0, Helm aye!

And here's an example of an incorrect response requiring a correction:

OOD: Helm, come right to course 1, 8, 0.
Helm: Come right to course 1, 5, 0, Helm aye!
OOD: Wrong! Come right to course 1, 8, 0.
Helm: Come right to course 1, 8, 0, Helm aye!

Note that with small numbers, everyone should say each digit individually to prevent confusion. Also note that in these examples, the order is directed at an individual, not just shouted to everyone on the Bridge.

Photo: Taken by me on my voyage on the USS Ronald Reagan

Air traffic control: When a controller provides instructions to a pilot, the pilot repeats the instructions to confirm that they have been received correctly.

Controller: "Fly heading 2, 7, 0, climb and maintain 10,000 feet."

The pilot Responds, "Fly heading 2, 7, 0, climb and maintain 10,000 feet."

Controller Confirmation: Roger, 2, 7, 0, climb and maintain 10,000 feet

Healthcare: When a nurse or doctor gives medication instructions to a patient, the patient repeats the instructions to confirm understanding.

The nurse Says: "Take one tablet of this medication with food twice a day."

The Patient Responds: "Take one tablet with food twice a day."

Nurse Confirmation: Yes, Take one tablet with food twice a day

Overall, the repeat-back process effectively confirms that information has been accurately transmitted and understood, reducing the risk of errors and improving safety in high-stakes environments.

How would this work in the pharmaceutical industry? A batch record requiring a critical or complex step to have a "Done-By" and "Verified-By" signature is a logical place to implement this repeat-back process.

When the repeat back process was implemented at Amgen within batch records, human errors were reduced by 98%.

Human Factors Design

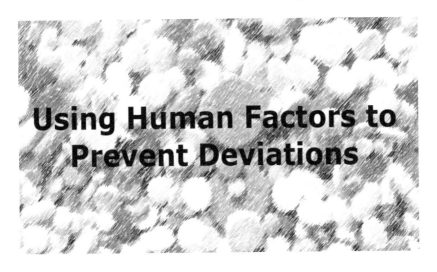

Human Factors Design is the practice of designing products, systems, or processes with the user in mind to optimize their effectiveness, safety, comfort, and efficiency. It considers the user's physical, cognitive, and emotional abilities and limitations and the environment in which the product or system will be used.

Human factors are used in a wide range of industries. In healthcare, for example, human factors design is used to design medical devices and equipment that are safe and effective to use, while in manufacturing, it is used to create workstations and processes that minimize physical strain and fatigue.

The goal of human factors is to create products and systems that are efficient, effective, and safe and that minimize the risk of error or injury.

By taking into account the needs and abilities of the user, human factors design can improve the usability and performance of products and systems and enhance the overall user experience.

So why not use human factors to write SOPs?

Incorporating human factors principles into SOPs can help ensure that the processes are safe, effective, and efficient. Here are some steps to help you use human factors to write SOPs:

- Before writing an SOP, you must identify who will use the process. This user identification will help you understand the user's needs, abilities, and limitations and help you design a process that is easy to follow and effective.
- The environment in which the process will be performed can also impact its effectiveness. For example, if the procedure is performed in a noisy or distracting environment, it may be necessary to design the process with additional safeguards to minimize errors.
- Use clear and straightforward language to make the SOP easy to understand and follow. Use visual aids, such as diagrams or flowcharts, to make the process easier to visualize.
- Use consistent formatting, such as headings, bullet points, and numbering, to make the SOP easy to read and follow. This formatting will also make it easier for users to locate specific steps or information.
- Get feedback from users on the SOP to ensure that it is easy to understand and follow. Incorporate any suggestions or input into the SOP to improve its effectiveness.

- Test the SOP to ensure that it is effective and efficient. This testing can involve conducting a dry run of the process to identify any areas that need improvement.
- SOPs should be reviewed and updated regularly to remain effective and relevant. This review is especially important if there are changes to the process or the user's environment.

By incorporating human factors principles into SOPs, you can design safer, more efficient, and more effective processes. In addition, this incorporation can help improve the overall quality of the work performed and reduce the risk of errors or accidents.

In summary, many tools can be used within the pharmaceutical industry to reduce human error. However, if circumstances lead to human errors, use one of the above tools or research other tools to allow individuals to achieve top-level performance, which benefits the individual and the organization.

Chapter 17 - Supplier Selection

I was once asked how to apply Phase Appropriate GMPs when selecting a supplier. I found the question interesting and decided to provide my views. Supplier selection is critical for any stage in a drug's lifecycle. I cannot imagine any company wanting a substandard supplier. As we all know, changing suppliers later in the lifecycle is time-consuming, resource-intensive, and could require FDA approval. There are many examples where drugs were not approved because a poor supplier was selected. I had a critical supplier go out of business (financially insolvent) just as the drug was undergoing FDA review for approval. What a disaster!

The FDA just issued a Warning Letter to an excipient supplier, so what will the consequences be to any drug approval applications pending FDA approval?

The most exciting experience involved a supplier who was an individual's friend within R&D, providing a critical reagent used in release testing that was approved in numerous regulatory approvals. This critical reagent was extremely expensive. Yet, one day, orders just stopped being filled. There was no communication from the supplier, and no one answered the phone at the supplier.

The supplier was about 100 miles away, so I got into the car and drove to the supplier's address, a small building next to a residential property. But unfortunately, when I knocked on the door, no one answered. So, I started to peer through the windows and saw what looked like a laboratory.

Eventually, a middle-aged woman came out of the house and asked if she could help me. I then explained the situation, and she started to cry. Once she composed herself, she explained that her husband owned the business and recently died unexpectedly.

She said her husband did not keep any records, and she could not figure out what to do.

We then went into the lab together, trying to figure out how to proceed forward. I eventually found a lab notebook with directions for making the critical reagent. I asked if I could take the notebook so we could continue to manufacture life-sustaining medication. The owner's widow agreed to let me take the notebook, and I decided that every time we prepared a batch of the critical reagent, we would pay her what we paid her husband.

What could have been a significant disaster turned into a win-win solution because I got off my ass and took some initiative.

Many advocate a risk-based approach to supplier selection. I'm afraid I have to disagree somewhat. However, even the corrugated box supplier cannot be ignored. Without corrugated box shipping containers, how does the medicine get to the patient who needs to be treated when they need to be treated? The level of GMP documentation, the frequency of audits, and what and how the items are tested upon receipt can change at various product lifecycle stages. However, when selecting a supplier, the supplier must be reliable, consistent, financially stable, and produce quality products at all stages of a lifecycle.

My advice when selecting and monitoring any supplier is to:

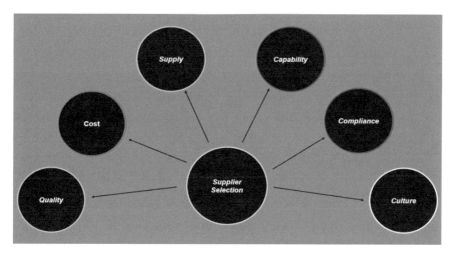

- Use external sources to provide data to assist your assessment.
- Identify potential risks associated with the supplier, such as product quality, regulatory compliance, supply chain management, financial stability, and their capability and capacity to support production volumes. For example, a supplier's capability and capacity involves evaluating if the supplier has the right technical talent to support your product and if the supplier has taken on more projects than they can adequately support.

- Evaluate the supplier's quality systems to ensure they comply with regulatory requirements and industry best practices. Review their quality control procedures, product testing methods, and product release criteria. This evaluation can be outsourced using a company like SQA Services, Inc.
- Check the supplier's compliance with regulatory requirements, such as GMP, GDP, and GCP. In addition, ensure they have the licenses, permits, and certifications required to operate. An excellent source for the inspection history is Redica Systems.
- Analyze the supplier's supply chain management, including transportation and storage practices, to identify potential product quality and safety risks.
- Review the supplier's financial stability, including cash flow, debt obligations, and credit rating. This review will help assess the supplier's ability to maintain production and supply continuity. Have the supplier provide you with their D-U-N-S number, and then use Dun and Bradstreet to evaluate many aspects of the supplier.
- Assess the supplier's contingency plans in the event of unforeseen circumstances, such as natural disasters, power outages, or product recalls.
- Review if the supplier is committed to continuous improvement and collaboratively working with your organization.

- Review communication and documentation: Review the supplier's communication and documentation processes, including their response times, clarity of communication, and documentation accuracy.
- Most importantly, does the supplier's culture mesh with your culture? For example, if the supplier is secretive and your organization is highly collaborative, the relationship will be bumpy, and no one will be satisfied.

Overall, evaluating risk using a supplier requires a systematic approach to identifying potential threats, assessing the supplier's capabilities, and developing contingency plans to mitigate any identified risks. In addition, regular monitoring and assessment of the supplier's performance can help ensure pharmaceutical products' ongoing quality and safety. I see no difference when selecting a supplier during Phase 1 or when a product is commercialized; however, periodic auditing frequency and amount of documentation required could differ.

Chapter 18 - Third-Party Audits

I am amazed that I still receive the following question.

Will regulators accept audits conducted using third-party auditors?

The EMA and FDA have publicly said that well-trained third-party auditors are acceptable.

FDA Statements: An FDA professional in Compliance said, "FDA is very much in favor of industry's cooperative efforts, such as Rx-360..."This individual stated, "Anytime we see these kinds of collaborative approaches by industry, we're very heartened by them." The individual also noted that each manufacturer must justify their audit approaches, whether using a company's resources or a combination of that and an external party such as Rx-360 or SQA Services.

PharmTech has an excellent article on "How to Implement Third-Party Audits."

EMA FAQ Response from their Website:

"The document 'guidance on the occasions when it is appropriate for competent authorities to conduct inspections at the premises of manufacturers of active substances used as starting materials', published as part of the Community procedures, states that it is expected that manufacturing-authorization holders will gain assurance that the active substances they use are manufactured in accordance with GMP through audit of the active-substance suppliers. Small manufacturers may not have the necessary expertise or resources to conduct their own audits.

An audit conducted by the manufacturing-authorisation holder itself should be integral to the manufacturer's quality-assurance system and subject to the basic GMP requirements, i.e., conducted by properly qualified and trained staff in accordance with approved procedures. It should be properly documented. These aspects can be inspected as necessary by the competent authorities.

If a third party is involved, the arrangements should be subject to Chapter 7 of the GMP guideline. There should be evidence that the contract-giver has evaluated the contract-acceptor with respect to the aspects described above.

All parties involved should be aware that audit reports and other documentation relating to the audit will be made available for inspection by the competent authorities if requested. This should normally provide sufficient assurance that the results of an audit carried out by the third party are credible, thus waiving the need for an audit conducted by the manufacturing-authorisation holder itself. However, it must also be satisfactorily demonstrated that there are no conflicts of interest."

In conclusion, I thought this question was answered ten years ago. However, I have been asked this question many times recently and thought I could help memorialize the answer in writing with this post. Third-party audit firms like SQA Services, Inc. or shared audit programs like Rx-360 are now widely used and tested by regulators. I recently had this exchange at a PDA Conference.

Chapter 19 - The Key Metric for Evaluating a Manufacturing Operation

So, how do you know that things are working correctly in manufacturing?

I have seen too many quality metrics used in the pharmaceutical industry. Here are some of the most common ones:

- Batch failure rate, deviations, non-conformances, and product quality complaints (this metric tracks the number of product quality complaints received from customers), yield, manufacturing cycle time, change control cycle time, batch rejection rate, audit/inspection findings, and adverse events.

A long time ago, I heard this story about when Pepsi purchased Taco Bell in 1978. Taco Bell was not big on metrics. However, Pepsi ruled by metrics and eventually developed over thirty metrics for each store to track and manage. Think about that! Asking a fast food store manager with limited resources in the late 1970s to collect and analyze data for over thirty metrics without computers was crazy. I contend that this is virtually impossible. To Pepsi's disbelief, sales and margins declined after implementing the new metrics. They then hired a leader who graduated from McDonald's University, who then explained that only four metrics were necessary for a successful fast food restaurant. Pepsi eventually understood that over thirty metrics might be too many, but four could never be enough.

So, Pepsi management did what many management teams do: they hired a consultant. The consultant concluded that only four metrics were required. Still, Pepsi management could not believe the findings and again hired another consulting firm, and again, the results confirmed the four necessary metrics.

Begrudgingly, Pepsi implemented the four metrics taught by McDonald's University, and coincidentally, over time, McDonald's started to add metrics for the store manager to implement.

Taco Bell also introduced the "Mystery Shoppers," which are paid to go into Taco Bell locations acting as customers, collecting data around the four metrics.

As a result, Taco Bell stores became so successful that the same-store sales climbed rapidly, eventually surpassing MacDonald's individual store sales.

What would frustrate you when you go to a fast food restaurant?

I assume you went to the fast food restaurant to get something fast. You want to get what you ordered. The food is prepared correctly, and the facility is clean.

The above expectations are precisely how the metric system was created.

The new metrics systems were called F.A.C.T.

F is for Fast: Speed of service.

A is for Accurate: Accuracy of the order.

C is for Clean: Cleanliness of the restaurant, including restrooms.

T is for Temperature. Hot food should be hot, and cold food should be cold.

Observing Taco Bell's success, McDonald's eventually reversed course and continued to grow globally.

The point of this story is that the number of metrics is not essential to analyze, monitor and improve quality, but picking the few right metrics is vital!

Here is some advice:

- Focus on what matters: Don't get bogged down in collecting and analyzing data that isn't critical. Instead, focus on relevant metrics that can help you make informed decisions.
- Keep it simple: Choose a few key metrics that can provide a clear picture of performance. On the other hand, too many metrics can be overwhelming and make it difficult to focus on what matters.
- Make metrics actionable: Metrics should be actionable, providing insights that can be used to improve performance. Choose metrics that provide actionable insights and can help you identify areas for improvement.

Therefore, I am promoting that Disposition Cycle Time is the essential quality metric. Many have asked why this metric is so important.

Disposition Cycle Time is also inappropriately known as Product Release Cycle Time. The Disposition Cycle Time metric measures both product release and rejection cycle times.

So why do I consider Disposition Cycle Times the essential and valuable metric?

This metric measures the efficiency of the entire manufacturing system. Think of the manufacturing system as a fine-tuned machine. A fine-tuned manufacturing system is like a well-orchestrated symphony. Just as a conductor carefully coordinates the timing and movements of each musician to produce a harmonious sound, a skilled operations manager must oversee the coordination of every aspect of a manufacturing system to achieve optimal efficiency and output. Each component of the system must be fine-tuned and synchronized to work together seamlessly, just as each musician in an orchestra must play their part perfectly for the music to come together. Just as a symphony can evoke strong emotions in listeners, a fine-tuned manufacturing system can produce high-quality products that meet or exceed customer expectations, leading to greater satisfaction and loyalty.

So, suppose Disposition Cycle Times are inconsistent or excessively long. In that case, it is an excellent indication that things could be out of control in manufacturing, the laboratories, or the Quality Unit and should be thoroughly investigated.

However, if Disposition Cycle Times are excellent, it does not necessarily mean everything runs like that fine-tuned machine. Different items should be evaluated before making that conclusion, like whether the metrics are being gamed or fraud is occurring.

Therefore, the Disposition Cycle Time is the first metric I look at when evaluating a pharmaceutical manufacturing plant. This metric has never failed me when considering new suppliers, CMOs, or acquisition targets. This cycle time metric is not the only one I look at, but it is the most important. Therefore, I recommend that all quality professionals and pharmaceutical executives consider my approach.

Chapter 20 - Competitive Quality & Regulatory Intelligence Is Essential

Gathering competitive intelligence in the pharmaceutical industry to run the business and increase sales is commonplace. However, gathering quality and regulatory intelligence in a sophisticated manner is not as common to shape and maintain the quality system. Therefore, I encourage the quality unit to conduct quality and regulatory intelligence. Competitive intelligence is essential for staying ahead of the curve and compliant. For example, at one of the companies where I worked, the Compliance Committee of the Board of Directors insisted that they got to review Quality/Regulatory Intelligence, such as one plant's inspection data compared to other internal plants and how the company compared to its peers. Some of the metrics we used were the number of observations per inspection day. Also, the Compliance Committee wanted to review how drug shortages and adverse regulatory events were correlated and how our performance compared to our peers.

The pharmaceutical industry is highly regulated, and failure to comply with regulatory requirements can result in significant fines, product recalls, and damage to a company's reputation. By reviewing regulatory intelligence, companies can stay updated with advances in quality techniques, changes in regulations, and guidelines to ensure that their products and operations remain compliant.

The pharmaceutical industry is highly competitive, and staying ahead is essential for success. By reviewing quality and regulatory intelligence, companies can identify opportunities to improve their products and operations and stay updated with industry trends and developments.

The industry is also subject to various risks, including product safety and efficacy, intellectual property infringement, and supply chain disruptions. By reviewing quality and regulatory intelligence, companies can identify and prioritize potential risks and take steps to mitigate them.

Industry constantly evolves, and innovation is essential for companies to remain competitive. By reviewing quality and regulatory intelligence, companies can identify innovative technologies, global regulatory requirements, and other opportunities for innovation. In addition, this intelligence helps quality leaders determine what their quality system is doing well and where to improve. Intelligence can also provide documented data to support continuous improvement or to prevent a significant adverse regulatory finding.

The Board, CEO, and I concluded that reviewing quality and regulatory intelligence is essential for companies in the pharmaceutical industry to remain compliant, competitive, and innovative and to manage risks effectively.

So, how does a company conduct quality and regulatory intelligence? Here are some steps you can take:

Look for industry publications, regulatory agency websites, market research reports, daily current events from news sources, and other information sources relevant to your company and its competitors. I would spend the first hour of my day searching for and reading such information. To make my searches easier, I would use Google Alerts for specific keywords and send me an e-mail each morning with the results.

Attend and volunteer at industry conferences and events to network with peers, learn about new products and services, and keep current with regulatory and quality trends. I dedicated part of my professional life to volunteering for professional organizations like the Parenteral Drug Association and eventually becoming a board member and the Board Chair. As a result, I made many valuable friends and connections that helped me and that I helped throughout my career.

Use online databases such as PubMed, Embase, and the FDA website to search for relevant information on drugs, clinical trials, and regulatory updates. I learned that my company already had subscriptions to these services, and I just needed to find the correct person to add me to the company subscription.

Engage with experts in the industry, such as consultants, regulatory affairs professionals, and quality assurance professionals, to gain insights and updates. I achieved this at various conferences and volunteer activities and through the friends I made over my career.

Utilize technology such as automated monitoring systems and data analytics tools to track and analyze regulatory and quality intelligence, such as Redica Systems.

Develop internal processes for monitoring and analyzing the competitive quality and regulatory landscape, including assigning roles and responsibilities, establishing metrics, and setting up regular reporting mechanisms.

Overall, gathering competitive quality and regulatory intelligence in the pharmaceutical industry requires a multifaceted approach that involves leveraging various sources of information and utilizing technology to stay current with the latest developments.

Several online databases can help gather competitive quality and regulatory intelligence in the pharmaceutical industry. Here are examples:

- Embase: A biomedical and pharmacological database that provides access to articles and abstracts from thousands of journals, conference proceedings, and other sources of information.
- FDA website: The US Food and Drug Administration (FDA) website provides information on drug approvals, recalls, safety alerts, and other regulatory updates.
- European Medicines Agency (EMA) website: The EMA website provides information on drug approvals, regulatory guidelines, and other regulatory updates for the European Union.

These databases gather information on drugs, clinical trials, regulatory updates, and other relevant topics in the pharmaceutical industry.

Several paid services are available for gathering competitive quality and regulatory intelligence in the pharmaceutical industry. Here are some examples:

- Redica Systems is a regulatory intelligence and analytics platform that provides real-time updates on regulatory changes, product approvals, and other industry news. Redica offers a range of features, including customizable alerts, search capabilities, and reporting tools.
- Pharma Intelligence is a suite of products offered by Informa, including news, analysis, and data on the pharmaceutical and biotechnology industries. In addition, it provides a range of features, including regulatory and clinical trial information, drug pipelines, and market analysis.
- Cortellis is a suite of products Clarivate Analytics offers, including drug pipeline, patent information, and regulatory and clinical trial data.
- GlobalData Healthcare is a research and analytics firm that provides insights and analysis on the healthcare industry, including the pharmaceutical and biotechnology sectors.
- Resilinc is a supply chain mapping organization. Resilinc scans over 100 languages, 200 countries, and 50 disruption types while AI removes the noise, so your alerts are 100% relevant. Resilinc experts then provide actionable notifications tailored to your unique business requirements.
- Sourcemap is a supply chain mapping organization that maps and monitors the end-to-end supply chain in line with US and EU due diligence requirements: forced labor, conflict minerals, counter-terrorism, anti-greenwashing, deforestation, etc.

120

These paid services can provide comprehensive and up-to-date information on regulatory and quality intelligence in the pharmaceutical industry but can be expensive. Therefore, it is essential to carefully evaluate the features and pricing of these services before deciding which one to use.

So, what do you do with this data? First, you have to communicate your findings and then build consensus and change what is required.

Communicating regulatory intelligence is essential to keep stakeholders informed about changes and updates in regulations and guidelines. Here are some tips for effectively communicating regulatory intelligence.

When communicating regulatory intelligence, it is crucial to tailor your message to your audience. Different stakeholders, such as regulatory affairs professionals, senior management, or external partners, may have distinct levels of expertise and interest in the topic.

Regulatory intelligence can be complex and technical, so communicating clearly and concisely is essential. Avoid jargon and technical terms that may not be familiar to all stakeholders.

When communicating regulatory intelligence, providing context and explaining why the information is important and vital. This information can help stakeholders understand the implications of regulatory changes and how they may affect the organization.

Visual aids like graphs and charts can effectively communicate regulatory intelligence. They can help stakeholders understand complex information more easily and quickly.

Regulatory intelligence is constantly evolving, so it is essential to update stakeholders regularly. This information can help ensure everyone is updated with the latest developments and can take appropriate action.

Use various communication methods to reach stakeholders, such as email, teleconferences, meetings, and presentations. This approach can help ensure that everyone receives the information in a format that works for them.

In summary, effective communication of regulatory intelligence requires tailoring your message to your audience, using clear and concise language, providing context, visual aids, regular updates, and multiple communication channels.

Implementing changes based on quality and regulatory intelligence can be a complex process and will depend on the specific context and needs of the organization. However, here are some general steps that can be taken to implement changes:

- Before implementing any changes, it is essential to assess the impact of regulatory intelligence on the organization. This assessment may involve reviewing current policies and procedures, evaluating the potential impact on products and operations, and identifying any resources required to implement the changes.

- Based on the assessment, develop a plan for implementing the changes. This plan may involve developing new policies and procedures, updating existing ones, and communicating the changes to stakeholders.
- Assign responsibilities for implementing the changes to specific individuals or teams within the organization. This approach may involve identifying subject matter experts who can provide guidance, support, and oversight throughout the process.
- Provide training: Provide training to employees who will be affected by the changes to ensure they understand the new policies and procedures and can implement them effectively.
- Implementing, monitoring, and evaluating their effectiveness is essential. This approach may involve conducting audits or assessments to ensure compliance, collecting stakeholder feedback, and adjusting as needed.
- Continuously review and update: Quality and regulatory intelligence are constantly evolving, so it is essential to continuously review and update policies and procedures to ensure ongoing compliance and effectiveness.

The following are examples of where practical regulatory and quality intelligence allowed risk mitigation plans to be developed or rapid response implemented that prevented several crises in my career:

- A fire at a chemical plant led to the unavailability of a critical raw material required to manufacture plastic components for medical devices. Learning of this fire promptly allowed us to procure enough existing raw material inventory for two years of manufacturing.
- Weather patterns in Canada affected the essential fatty acid profiles in soybean and safflower oils used to manufacture intravenous fat emulsions. Essential fatty acid profiles are a required specification, so watching the weather determines inventory needs two years into the future.
- Labor stoppages in the upstream supply chain have resulted in drug shortages. As a result, some companies monitor your upstream supply chain for such events and even notify you of pending labor negotiations.
- There were three natural disasters where supply chain mapping prevented drug shortages. Hurricane Maria devastated many suppliers in Puerto Rico, leading to a significant shortage of intravenous saline. A volcanic eruption in Iceland shut down air travel in the northern hemisphere, causing major supply change disruptions for over a month. Finally, an earthquake led to a tsunami in Japan that impacted the pharmaceutical supply chain.

- Identifying regulatory compliance issues quickly within the supply chain or with other pharmaceutical companies allowed me to take preventative actions or quick adjustments to minimize the impact we experienced.

In summary, quality and regulatory intelligence is essential and can be easily achieved using numerous sources. Implementing changes requires assessing the impact, developing a plan, assigning responsibilities, providing training, monitoring and evaluating, and continuously reviewing and updating policies and procedures.

Chapter 21 - Quality Personnel on the Floor

Let me start by saying again that quality is everyone's responsibility, not just that of quality professionals. Having said that…

I have always insisted on having Quality Unit (QU) personnel on the shop floor for several reasons. First and foremost, they are accountable per regulations in ensuring that products meet the required quality and compliance standards. It continuously reinforces the value of a quality organization. Here are other benefits of QU personnel on the floor:

- QU personnel on the shop floor ensure that products meet the required regulatory standards. In addition, they ensure that the products are manufactured following established quality procedures and specifications.
- QU personnel can conduct real-time batch record reviews, which prevent simple documentation errors that lead to nuisance non-conformances. Reviewing the batch records contemporaneously, page by page, on the shop floor means there is no need for an additional Quality Unit review weeks after the product is produced. This contemporaneous review catches problems in real-time, allows for immediate corrections, improves the speed of the product disposition process, and ensures that the product is formulated correctly.

- Quality Unit personnel on the shop floor are trained to identify defects and potential problems during manufacturing. Identifying these issues early can prevent them from becoming more significant problems later on, which would be more expensive to correct or lead to batch rejects and recalls.
- QU personnel can prevent problems in-process to be dealt with correctly due to time pressures to meet schedules. For example, I have seen minor, inexpensive in-process errors forward-processed due to time pressures, resulting in expensive rejected or recalled batches. Time pressure in manufacturing is a significant cause of bad decisions, and having QU personnel on the shop floor helps mitigate this risk.
- QU personnel can work with other teams to develop and implement quality improvement initiatives, which leads to better products.

It is vital in selecting who is the Quality individual on the floor. These individuals must know the manufacturing process; these individuals are more of a coach than police. In other words, a quality professional and not a compliance professional.

It is essential to remember that quality is the responsibility of everyone. Having "QU personnel on the shop floor" is not a waiver for the quality responsibilities of the manufacturing personnel. Quality is built into products by those in manufacturing.

When I decided that the Quality Unit had to be on the shop floor when production was underway, it was an unpopular decision with the Quality Unit personnel. These jobs were no longer:

- 9 to 5, five days a week job;
- in an office environment and
- some quality professionals felt a loss of status.

There will always be resistance from senior management, McKinsey-type consultants, and others about cost and waste. However, they might change their minds if they take the time to look at the data. The data demonstrate fewer documentation errors, elimination of time pressure costly mistakes, and faster product disposition cycle times.

I had to continue to push one of my plant quality managers to implement quality of the floor, including contemporaneous batch record review. I visited this plant about once every 2 to 3 months. For about a year, on every visit, I had to continue to push for quality on the floor.

I eventually informed the quality manager that the next time I visited the plant, if he had not implemented quality on the floor, I would have maintenance remove his office furniture from his office. Before my visit, I verified that he did not implement quality on the floor, so he lost his office and did not get it back until quality on the floor was implemented.

Overall, having quality personnel on the shop floor is essential in ensuring that products meet the required quality standards, improving efficiency, reducing costs, enhancing customer satisfaction, and ensuring safety.

Chapter 22 - Don't Overload the System With Junk

I have seen this far too many times. That every event (deviation or non-conformance is treated identically. Valuable and scarce resources investigate non-consequential events with no patient safety risks with the same vigor as the most significant non-conformances. If they were to reoccur and escape the quality system, they could seriously harm a patient.

When I joined a company, they treated every event precisely the same when investigating, which resulted in a significant backlog of investigations. Even after being repeatedly told by the regulators that what they were doing was unacceptable, no changes were made, and they continued to add to the backlog of investigations.

This situation is where a leader separates themselves from a manager. The manager will try to manage the situation and may make tweaks around the edges to improve. A leader will evaluate the situation and propose drastic changes that differ from the existing approach, which may not be popular. The leader has to be willing to put their job on the line to make such drastic changes.

As a leader, you must have the team focus on the most critical items while not ignoring minor or nuisance events. So, how do you apply this to deviations and nonconformances?

The first step is assembling a cross-functional team of subject matter experts to develop a risk matrix to evaluate all previous investigations, and categorizing them using a Failure Mode and Effects Analysis (FMEA) to calculate a Risk Priority Number (RPN). The following criteria should be used in the FMEA:

- Frequency of the event
- Ability to Detect the Event
- Risk to the Patient if the Event is Not Detected

FMEA worksheet

Project:
Product:
System: ①

Date:
Prepared by: ②

FMEA Number:: ③
Reference documents:

System / Component / Function	Potential Failure mode	Potential effect(s) of failure	Severity	Critical?	Potential cause(s) of failure	Occurrence	Current design controls	Detection	Risk Priority Number	Recommended action(s)	Responsibility & completion date
④	⑤	⑥	⑦	⑧	⑨	⑩	⑪	⑫	⑬	⑭	⑮

Then, it is important to memorialize the results and categorization of each type of event in a Standard Operating Procedure. The next step is to determine how many levels of investigation are required. I suggest three levels: Class 1, Class 2, and Class 3; High, Medium, and Low; or Critical, Major, and Minor, as the MHRA (Medicines and Healthcare Products Regulatory Agency) does with their Inspectional Observations. Then, clearly prescribe what is required for each category of event. Finally, routinely audit how events are classified to ensure compliance with the procedure.

I can't stress the importance of these audits enough.

You will be surprised at what you find. Individuals tend to "upgrade" the classification, fearing the FDA might challenge their grading. As a leader, you must insist that the company procedure is followed.

Starting with the lowest risk grade (Minor): Document the event in the system, make the responsible individuals aware that the event was recorded in the quality system, and close the Minor Investigation. I am not saying to ignore the event; it should be tracked, trended, and if the event type is too frequent or increasing in frequency, investigate why and implement corrective actions.

Medium Risk (Major): Conduct a thorough investigation after finding probable root causes and implement corrective actions.

High Risk (Critical): Consider if the operation must be shut down. If no shutdown is necessary, an interim investigation report must be issued within 30 days, followed by monthly reports, concluding that manufacturing can continue or cease operation until the investigation is closed.

A Critical Investigation should find the true root cause and implement preventive and corrective actions.

Using precise language within an investigation is essential since regulators could thoroughly review them. What do I mean by appropriate language? Don't use unique company abbreviations, slang, or inflammatory terms. For example, in the event description, don't say the product failed the specification. Instead, state that you are investigating an out-of-specification result. If you lead with the statement that the product failed, no matter what the investigation uncovers and documents, you have already determined that the product must be rejected.

Many regulatory investigators will ask for a list of all investigations, including a description of the event and disposition of the product.

So if the list generated for the investigator says the product failed the specification and disposition states the product should be released, which makes no sense. Therefore, that investigation will be thoroughly reviewed since failing a specification should be an automatic rejection. It is much better to describe the event as the test result was not within the prescribed range. Replace words like "issue" with "event"; "failure' with "anomaly"; inevitably, you will be challenged by a tiered approach to events.

135

These challenges will be well intended but must be addressed promptly and with conviction. Usually, these challenges are from within the company, worried about what FDA investigators will think and whether this will lead to significant inspectional observations.

Then, there will be individuals who act out of fear and will classify things correctly but do more than required per the procedure for that level of investigation, which will compromise the entire event rating system. On the other hand, others will increase the significance level of the event to do more investigative work, violating their training and procedure.

Therefore, solid metrics and internal audits are required to ensure the procedures are followed correctly. Here are some metric guidelines:

Type of Event	Percentage of All Events	Time to Close
Critical	Less than a Few Percent	90 Days or Greater
Major	Less Than 25%	Not More Than 30 Days
Minor	More than 75%	Not More than 5 Days

Have you caught my error in the language I used above? Why would you classify an investigation as "Critical" even before an investigation is started?

Here are my final words on this topic and an excellent position in discussions with naysayers. Ask how many open and backlogged investigations they have. Then, ask how many of those investigations would be considered critical for patient safety. Then, ask them why they are investigating a minor event with no patient safety consequence when critical events with patient safety consequences remain open and older than 30 days.

Chapter 23 - Make it Easy to Comply

It is easy to say that you will comply and that your job depends on it. But as a leader, your job is to make it easier to comply than not.

Making compliance easier involves a deliberate effort to simplify processes, improve communication, and create a supportive environment for individuals and organizations to meet their obligations.

Far too many times, individuals make it hard to comply with the GMPs. The number one reason individuals and organizations make it hard to comply is trying to be perfect. Here are some suggestions on how to make it easy to comply.

Here are some simple and clear instructions to make compliance easier:

- Make sure the instructions are easy to understand and free from ambiguity.
- Simplified Forms and Reporting: Minimize the required fields in compliance forms and reports. Use pre-filled information whenever possible to save time and effort for those complying.
- Provide necessary resources: Ensure people can access all the tools, equipment, or resources needed to complete the task.
- Remove obstacles: Identify and eliminate any barriers that could hinder compliance. Simplify processes and get rid of unnecessary steps.

- Educate and communicate: Clearly explain the importance of compliance and provide information about why it matters.
- Automate tasks: Use automation to reduce the workload and increase efficiency.
- Seek feedback: Ask for feedback to understand challenges and gather suggestions for improvement.
- Be flexible: Allow different approaches to achieve compliance to accommodate individual needs and circumstances.

Always consider the specific situation and the people involved when implementing these strategies. With these steps, compliance should become more manageable and straightforward for everyone.

As a quality leader, I was also responsible for Environmental Health and Safety. Here is an excellent example where the company made it hard for technicians to comply and work safely.

One day, I received a call that a technician was burned from an electrical shock while working on an HVAC unit. The investigation revealed that an HVAC unit outside of a building located at the bottom of a stairwell to the basement was involved in the safety incident. To de-energize the HVAC unit, the electrician had to climb a ship's ladder to the roof and walk across the entire length of the building's roof to enter a mechanical room to de-energize the HVAC unit. So one day, a technician needed to make a quick repair, and rather than go to extensive effort to de-energize the HVAC unit, he decided to make the fast repair while the HVAC unit was energized, and then boom! He shocked himself, burned his arm, and damaged the HVAC unit.

How hard would installing an electrical disconnect next to the HVAC unit have been? If this simple engineered solution were in place, it would make it easy for the technician to comply, preventing the safety incident.

When I joined a company as a senior quality executive, an individual came to my office to approve an SOP. I looked at the signature page, and my signature was the last of 27 approval signatures. The drive for perfection and not making a mistake leads to bureaucracy and discourages updating SOPs or making process improvements, thus making compliance hard.

Chapter 24 - Achieving Six Sigma Performance: So that Quality is Free

First, this is not a theory but is based on real-life experiences and implementations. I also want to share that this could not have happened without the partnership with my colleagues, the Head of Manufacturing, the Head of Product Development, and The Head of Operations.

Since we did not have many significant problems to address, I first needed to spend a great deal of time researching, collecting data, and demonstrating the value of improving product quality to 6 Sigma levels and how this would lower manufacturing costs. There would be no argument that enhancing the quality to these levels and reducing regulatory compliance risk to even lower levels would be nice to have. The test would be to convince leadership that it was worth the effort.

A well-characterized drug, robust manufacturing process, and reliable analytical methods are required to achieve Six Sigma performance. Everyone in R&D and Product Development believes they delivered this to manufacturing. Of course, manufacturing will swear that their processes are robust and analytical development will attest that their methods are accurate and relatable. So why are there failures?

Constant process monitoring and data collection are required to answer the robustness question. Most companies can collect the data without any resistance. Properly analyzing the data and implementing corrective actions is where the rubber hits the road, and resistance begins.

As part of our management review program, leaders of all three organizations, Quality, Manufacturing, and Product Development, met and reviewed the data collected for each product attribute we measured for raw materials, in-process monitoring, and with the finished product. We had the data crunched and reported out as performance in Sigmas. At this point, the organization was still on board.

Then, we assigned someone to be responsible for any attribute not performing above 1 Sigma to determine what was occurring and begin a process improvement program. It is important to note that, most likely, no product failures had occurred, but this was part of a process improvement plan.

These individuals would report their findings monthly to the expanded leadership team, including Compliance and Regulatory, for encouragement, resources, or to complain.

Individuals resisted taking on these assignments since they wanted to do more R&D. There were few failures, and they were hoping that if they waited long enough, the program would go away. Initially, there was much finger-pointing that this was not my problem; look over there, we can't make any changes because of the FDA and every other excuse you could imagine. For a long time, these monthly meetings were ugly. Many arguments broke out, voices were raised, and tempers flared. We even had individuals assigned to various issues who did not attend the meetings. So, at times, directives had to be issued. Eventually, the organizations accepted that this was not going away; it was part of their jobs, and they needed to excel here to be successful.

To get this program up and running, a united front from the heads of Quality, Manufacturing, Product Development, and Operations was critical and made a big difference. No one had a place to hide!

This program is one example of a bold initiative where the Head of Quality had to promote the value of this approach and sell it to leadership. Once that occurred, the Head of Manufacturing and, subsequently, the Head of Operations led the meeting.

Eventually, our persistence paid off, and root causes were identified; corrective actions were developed and implemented. This approach virtually eliminated all root causes, leading to less than 1 Sigma performance.

Based on the successes, the program was expanded to include parameters not meeting 3 Sigma. After those successes, the results were looked at in Pareto Charts, and the lower-performing opportunities were addressed.

The program was successful as it led to many attributes performing well above 6 Sigma, leading to fewer in-process and batch failures, investigations, etc. It even produced such convincing data that regulators allowed numerous inspections and testing requirements to be removed from the marketing authorization and discontinued.

These results were only achieved because the leadership team was convinced of the value and worked hard to make it happen.

Chapter 25 - Connecting the Dots

Later in my career, one of my friends, mentor, and supervisor once stated that I have the most incredible ability to connect the dots. What did he mean when he said that?

Connecting the dots relates to finding connections between seemingly unrelated ideas or information. I was able to do this to predict events that would impact the organization, such as supplier issues, regulatory changes, and current trends in the industry.

Here are some tips to help you connect the dots:

- Keep an open mind. Be receptive to the latest ideas and information and look at things from different perspectives.
- Look for patterns. Try to identify patterns or recurring themes in the information you have. Look for similarities and differences between ideas.
- Ask many questions. First, ask yourself questions about the information you have. What does it mean? How is it related to other ideas or information? What are the implications?
- Keep notes, articles, and documents. Keep track of your ideas and observations in a notebook or journal. This process can help you see connections over time and organize your thoughts.
- Attend professional meetings and seminars.
- Network with individuals within your area of expertise and with individuals from non-related and diverse industries.

- Seek out diverse sources of information. Look for information from various sources, including books, articles, videos, and individuals with diverse backgrounds and experiences. For example, I would spend the first hour of each morning looking at the competitive intelligence mentioned previously, reading about regulatory and industry events from online sources like Becker's and everyday current events from a news aggregator like Flipboard to build a diverse knowledge base to draw on while performing my job.
- Use and create analogies. Use analogies to help you understand and explain complex ideas. In addition, metaphors can help you make connections between seemingly disparate ideas.
- Try out the latest ideas and see how they fit with other information. Experimentation can help you uncover connections and new insights.

Connecting the dots requires creativity, curiosity, and persistence. You can see connections and make sense of complex information by staying open-minded, seeking out diverse sources, and asking questions.

I have used the following story in delivering several commencement speeches about connecting the dots.

The following anecdote is widely available online and in various publications. The story's source is Jobs' commencement speech at Stanford University in 2005, which is available on the Stanford University website and YouTube.

Steve Jobs, the co-founder of Apple, was known for his ability to connect the dots and see the bigger picture. In his famous Stanford University commencement speech in 2005, Jobs shared a story about how he learned to connect the dots in his own life.

https://news.stanford.edu/2005/06/12/youve-got-find-love-jobs-says/

He told a story about his adoption and how his birth mother was a graduate student who placed Steve up for adoption but insisted that his adoptive parents were college graduates. When he was born, the selected parents - a lawyer and his wife - decided they wanted a girl and backed out of the adoption. The next available parents on the waiting list were working-class parents who agreed to adopt Steve but had to promise his birth mother that he would attend college.

Seventeen years later, he naively chose a college as expensive as Stanford. After six months, he could not see the value in it. He had no idea what he wanted to do with his life or how college would help him figure it out. So, Steve dropped out of college but stayed around for a time, dropping in on classes that he would have never taken to obtain his degree. One of these classes was calligraphy, where he learned about the beauty of typefaces, letter spacing, and what makes typography great.

None of this had even a hope of any practical application in his life.

But ten years later, when designing the first Macintosh, he created all he learned, including calligraphy, into the Macintosh. As a result, it was the first computer with beautiful typography, and since Windows just copied the Macintosh, all computers today have beautiful typography.

Of course, it was impossible to connect the dots looking forward when he was in college. But it was clear looking backward years later.

He concludes, "You cannot connect the dots looking forward; you can only connect them looking backward. So, you must trust that the dots will somehow connect in the future. You must trust in something — your gut, destiny, life, karma, whatever."

The lesson of Steve Jobs' story is that every experience we have, no matter how small or seemingly irrelevant, can help us connect the dots and find our way in life. By staying open-minded, pursuing our passions, and trusting in our instincts, we can create a path that leads to success and fulfillment.

Chapter 26 - How I Solve Complex Problems

Solving complex problems is challenging, but there are helpful strategies.

First, I think to myself. Have I ever seen this or a similar problem before? Do I know someone else that might have seen a similar problem? Have I read or seen a presentation about a comparable situation? Did I hear or read about something similar outside the pharmaceutical industry? Then, what did I learn from those experiences? What did not go well, and what did I learn from those experiences? This process is just a small way I would connect the dots!

The importance of small steps

I find it essential to break the problem down into smaller parts. Complex problems involve multiple sub-problems. Breaking the problem into smaller parts allows me to focus on individual components and work toward a solution. I have found that solving just one of the parts can solve a sizable portion of the problem.

Most importantly, I never let perfection become the enemy of good. As a quality leader, this might be the most challenging part of the job: having to convince the quality organization to implement and deliver the goods quickly and not strive for perfection. Individuals who migrate to a quality disposition accept this approach, and those who migrate to a compliance disposition insist on perfection.

The quality leader needs to persuade both groups to implement a good part of a perfect solution in a step-wise fashion, which is best for quality and compliance.

I clearly define the problem, which involves identifying the potential root causes, understanding the scope of the problem, and defining the outcome.

I then gather as much relevant information as possible. This approach may involve researching, drawing on past experiences, or interviewing others.

Once I have gathered information, I analyze it to identify patterns, relationships, and potential solutions.

Based on my analysis, I will generate a list of viable solutions. I find it helpful to brainstorm and develop as many ideas as possible.

I evaluate each solution against the criteria I defined. This approach helps me to determine which solutions are viable and which are not.

Before implementing any solution, I think about the unintended consequences if the solution developed does not work. What could additionally go wrong and monitor for those events?

I ask myself if the proposed solution is like entering a one-way door through which there is no return or a two-way door through which I can return.

A one-way solution is a solution that is irreversible or difficult to reverse once it has been made. Once a one-way solution is implemented, it is difficult or impossible to change or undo. For example, once equipment has been removed and destroyed, it can be difficult to undo that solution.

On the other hand, a two-way solution is a decision that can be easily reversed or changed if it is not working out as planned. For example, if a procedure or process is modified and not working as well as I thought, I can easily switch back to the previous procedure or process and try another approach.

Implementing a one-way solution requires much more thought, preparation, and focus on execution. In addition, one-way solutions require more careful consideration and planning, as they are more difficult to undo or change. On the other hand, two-way decisions can be more flexible but still require care and planning.

Once I have identified a viable solution, the solution needs to be implemented. Again, decisiveness is critical; analysis paralysis or procrastination will only worsen things. This approach may involve acting, making changes, or communicating the solution to others.

After implementing the solution, I monitor its effectiveness and adjust as needed. This monitoring will help ensure that the solution continues to be effective over time.

Remember that solving complex problems can take time and effort. Therefore, it is essential to remain patient and persistent in finding a solution.

Chapter 27 - The Pharmaceutical Supply Chain

Before I begin, I have changed my views on globalization. I think the unintended consequences have far exceeded any benefits we have experienced here in the United States.

Rather than the supply chain being simple, robust, and resilient, it is a complex global network of suppliers, manufacturers, distributors, wholesalers, and retailers responsible for delivering safe and effective medicines to patients. The resulting supply chain is often complex, weak, and fragile. The only proof we need is to look at the number of critical drug shortages or the number of FDA actions against substandard suppliers in foreign countries. In addition, the increasing globalization and outsourcing of the pharmaceutical industry have made the supply chain more vulnerable to various threats, including counterfeiting, theft, diversion, and contamination. These challenges jeopardize public health and harm pharmaceutical companies' reputations and financial stabilities. Therefore, it is essential to have robust and transparent systems in place to monitor, mitigate, and prevent supply chain risks.

During the COVID pandemic, to overcome the weakness within the pharmaceutical supply chain, legislators, regulators, industry, and healthcare providers engaged in heroic efforts to ensure critical drugs, devices, and diagnostics were available to treat hospitalized patients, especially in areas where a large number of cases were overwhelming the system. These same types of heroic efforts also developed, approved, distributed and vaccinated over one hundred million Americans and six billion individuals globally.

One of the critical strategies for securing the pharmaceutical supply chain is the adoption of global standards and guidelines covering various aspects of pharmaceutical manufacturing, distribution, and storage. These standards and guidelines provide a common framework for ensuring product quality, safety, and efficacy, and they are essential for achieving regulatory compliance and market access. Another approach to securing the pharmaceutical supply chain is through technology and data analytics, such as serialization and track-and-trace technologies that allow manufacturers, distributors, and regulators to monitor the movement of products throughout the supply chain. Furthermore, data analytics can help stakeholders identify patterns and trends in supply chain data, detect potential risks, and make informed decisions to mitigate those risks.

Collaboration and information sharing among stakeholders are also critical for securing the pharmaceutical supply chain. Organizations such as Rx-360, a non-profit international consortium of pharmaceutical and biotech companies, suppliers, and regulators, promote collaboration and information sharing to enhance the integrity of the supply chain.

In 2009, I founded Rx-360, a supply chain professional organization, in collaboration with other global quality leaders in response to the intentional adulteration of heparin for economic gain. Heparin is a blood thinner, also known as an anticoagulant, used for many different indications where it is necessary to decrease the clotting ability of the blood and help prevent harmful clots from forming in blood vessels. The "crude" heparin was adulterated in China with oversulfated chondroitin sulfate and is responsible for killing patients worldwide.

Regulatory oversight is another essential element of securing the pharmaceutical supply chain. Regulatory authorities ensure medicines' safety, efficacy, and quality. These authorities establish and enforce regulations and guidelines that govern various aspects of the pharmaceutical supply chain, such as GMPs, GDPs (Good Distribution Practices), and product quality standards. They also conduct inspections and audits to ensure compliance with these regulations and guidelines and take enforcement actions when necessary.

Securing the pharmaceutical supply chain is a complex and multifaceted task that requires a combination of strategies and solutions. Adopting global standards and guidelines, using technology and data analytics, promoting collaboration and information sharing, and ensuring regulatory oversight are all essential components of a robust and resilient supply chain. By working together, stakeholders can help to prevent supply chain risks, ensure the safety and efficacy of medicines, and ultimately, protect public health.

I suggest that all pharmaceutical and healthcare professionals read two books; "Bottle of Lies" by Katherine Eban and "China Rx" by Rosemary Gibson.

"Bottle of Lies" is a non-fiction book by investigative journalist Katherine Eban, which examines the dark side of the generic drug industry. The book reveals how some of India's largest generic drug manufacturers have been falsifying data, cutting corners on safety and quality, and engaging in other unethical practices to increase profits. The author exposes the flaws in the regulatory system that allowed these practices to persist and provides a detailed account of the efforts of whistleblowers, investigators, and regulators to expose these issues. As a result, the book sheds light on a crucial point that affects public health and safety, as well as the integrity of the pharmaceutical industry. Overall, "Bottle of Lies" is a compelling and well-researched exposé that raises essential questions about the safety and efficacy of generic drugs.

"China Rx" is a non-fiction book by investigative journalist Rosemary Gibson that explores the dependence of the United States on China for its pharmaceutical supply. The book reveals how China has become the world's leading supplier of pharmaceuticals, including essential medicines such as antibiotics, and the potential dangers of this reliance. The authors document cases of contamination, substandard and counterfeit drugs, and regulatory failures that have put patients at risk.

They also highlight the lack of transparency and accountability in the pharmaceutical supply chain and the need for reform. Overall, "China Rx" is a well-researched and alarming account of the vulnerabilities of the US healthcare system and the urgent need for action to address this critical issue.

Based on the events described above, in the books "Bottle of Lies" and "China Rx" and others to be discussed later in the book, many pharmaceutical companies and national governments are seriously considering reshoring the pharmaceutical supply chains. For example, BARDA (U.S. Government Biomedical Advanced Research and Development Authority) awarded Phlow and Civica Rx a multimillion-dollar award. Phlow is a public-benefit active pharmaceutical ingredient development and manufacturing company. Civica Rx is a non-profit pharmaccutical company that re-shores essential generic medications in the United States. Phlow and Civica Rx are creating in one location a short-simple-robust-resilient supply chain from R&D to finished products, including active ingredient and their precursors.

Chapter 28 - Drug Shortages
The High Costs of Cheap Drugs

Drug shortages have plagued the healthcare system for over a decade. As I write this book, there are over 300 drug shortages in the United States that impact patient care. So, after I retired, I decided to take on drug shortages. There are several reasons why drug shortages occur. One reason is that the demand for a particular drug may exceed the supply. This increase in demand can happen if there is an unexpected increase in the number of patients who need the medication or if the drug is required to treat a disease outbreak or pandemic. Another reason is that supply chain disruptions may prevent the drug from being produced or distributed. These disruptions can happen with natural disasters, transportation problems, or manufacturing issues. In addition, regulatory issues can also cause drug shortages. For example, if a drug manufacturer is required to change its manufacturing process or labeling, it may temporarily halt drug production, resulting in a shortage.

Finally, the primary cause of drug shortages is economic factors that can also play a role in drug shortages. If a drug becomes less profitable for manufacturers, they may discontinue production, leading to shortages. Most generic drugs have five to ten companies authorized to provide a particular generic. However, over time as the price of generic drugs erode, companies stop producing drugs that are not economically viable, and only one or two companies might be left producing a particular drug, making the drug susceptible to drug shortages.

Dr. Robert Califf's resounding declaration regarding the prevailing drug shortages in the United States goes beyond the realm of healthcare – it pierces through to the very core of national security. As the FDA commissioner, his authority amplifies his message, emphasizing the gravity of the situation. It's not merely a matter of supply and demand but of safeguarding our country's stability and well-being.

With an acute understanding of the complexities of the pharmaceutical landscape, Califf's call to action takes center stage. He calls upon drug companies, pivotal players in this intricate web, to proactively address the looming crisis. By establishing a robust communication channel with the FDA, these companies can provide early warnings about potential shortages. This collaborative approach isn't just about mitigating the immediate fallout; it's about fortifying the foundation upon which our healthcare system stands.

Califf's astute analysis uncovers a crucial linchpin of the shortages: the decline in the production of generics. The equilibrium is disrupted in a landscape where the pricing pendulum wildly swings, with exorbitant costs characterizing the "innovator industry" and minimal pricing marking the generic side. His argument prompts a deeper examination of the pricing dynamics, suggesting that a harmonious balance could be instrumental in averting future shortages.

Peering through the lens of history, Califf's observations unveil a recurring theme: manufacturing issues as a historical culprit behind drug shortages. This historical perspective serves as a cautionary tale, urging us to confront these issues with strategic foresight. By addressing manufacturing bottlenecks and challenges, we take a significant step toward preventing future shortages.

Within this intricate tapestry of shortages, Califf singles out the oncology sector as a matter of immediate concern. The urgency of the oncology shortage is palpable, making Califf's call for drug companies to promptly alert the FDA even more pertinent. This sector, where timely access to medications is a matter of life and death, accentuates the overarching narrative that the implications of these shortages are far-reaching and deeply personal.

Amidst the complexity, Califf's admission that certain aspects of drug shortages might be "out of our control" acknowledges the multifaceted nature of the issue. Yet, his acknowledgment is not a call for resignation; it's an appeal for collective responsibility. By uniting stakeholders – regulatory bodies, drug companies, healthcare providers, and the public – we confront this challenge with a united front, determined to carve a path forward.

In embracing the entirety of Califf's insights, it becomes evident that his message transcends the boundaries of healthcare regulation. It speaks to the resilience of a nation, the commitment to its citizens' well-being, and the collaborative effort needed to preserve both. The urgency of his call is matched only by the potential of a united response – a response that could redefine how we safeguard our healthcare landscape and, by extension, our national security.

We should expect drug shortages to get worse. But, unfortunately, it is too late to prevent drug shortages, and we are reaping what we have sown. By allowing essential generic medicines to become commodities and the pharmaceutical supply chain to globalize, mainly leaving the United States, we have created the perfect environment for developing drug shortages.

Essential medications needed to treat the terribly sick are the old standbys, such as antibiotics, diuretics, antihypertensives, and sedation agents. Approximately 3 of 4 essential medications do not have a United States source for the active ingredients. As a society, we encouraged the price to be driven down to unsustainable levels ("The Race to the Bottom"). For example, some sterile injectables sell for $0.39 a vial, and most essential medicines are sold for less than $2 (U.S.) per container. As Janet Woodcock, MD, Director of the Center for Drug Evaluation and Research, has stated, "Why is it acceptable that we expect essential sterile injectable medicines to cost less than a Starbucks coffee?"

These meager prices have turned essential medicines into commodities, like oil. When oil prices fall too low, oil exploration and pumping oil out of the ground halts, resulting in shortages and rapid price increases. Why should we expect anything different for essential medications from the broken economic model we created? This fractured model creates problems beyond the ability of most units within a company to fix, including Quality, R&D, Engineering, and Manufacturing. These units cannot fix the shortage problem because they cannot address the actual root cause. These conclusions of a broken economic model have also been validated in the most recent FDA drug shortage report, "Drug Shortages: Root Causes and Potential Solutions, Published in October 2019."

This broken economic model has forced the pharmaceutical supply chains to become long, complex, and fragile to reduce costs, creating a dependency on foreign countries for our pharmaceuticals, especially China. It has been reported that 80% of drugs depend on raw materials, active pharmaceutical ingredient precursors, active pharmaceutical ingredients, and even drug products from China.

In addition, at unsustainably low prices, there is little appetite for investment in sterile filling capacity, upgrading existing facilities, or making process improvements; instead, the available capacity is used for the most profitable products, such as branded pharmaceuticals, biotech medicines, or biosimilars. There is also reduced investment in facility maintenance, supplier development, and product quality. The result is a complex pharmaceutical supply chain that is long and fragile, depending heavily on India and China.

As mentioned before, two excellent books, "Bottle of Lies: The Inside Story of the Generic Boom" by Kathrine Eban and "China Rx: Exposing the Risks of America's Dependence on China for Medicine" by Rosemary Gibson, clearly describes the risks and results of globalization on the pharmaceutical supply chain. These are excellent reads for anyone in the pharmaceutical and healthcare industries. Bottle of Lies focuses on the inferior quality and data integrity issues at certain Indian manufacturers. China Rx focuses on national security issues regarding allowing China to become the world's pharmacy.

Here are some interesting and scary facts from a ZEMBLA Documentary https://youtu.be/z6MtJSo_CAY

- Most of the world's antibiotics come from China
- All of the world's doxycycline and rifampin come from China
- Five of the most effective oncology agents are made by just one Chinese Company
- 80% of all active pharmaceutical ingredients depend on a precursor provided by China

Based on the short-term success that the generic drug industry had with globalizing its supply chains, many branded pharmaceutical companies have followed suit. However, even if the active pharmaceutical ingredients are produced in the U.S. or Europe, one must ask where the chemical precursors required to manufacture the active pharmaceutical ingredients are sourced.

During COVID, India has prohibited exporting 26 active pharmaceutical ingredients or medications. Other countries will likely follow suit in the future to protect their citizens.

I had the honor to start and lead the non-profit generic drug company Civica Rx, created by leading U.S. health systems and philanthropies to address drug shortages. Civica's unique business model is nothing proprietary or earth-shattering, but it costs money and takes resources to launch and achieve rapid success. For-profit, generic drug companies prefer not to implement the Civica Rx model because it significantly adds to their operating costs.

Here are the key initiatives initiated by Civica to prevent drug shortages of essential generic medications for our more than 1,500 hospital members that continues to expand.

- Create long-term guaranteed contracts between health systems, Civica, and our suppliers.
- Don't buy active pharmaceutical ingredients from China or India when possible; invest in shortening the complex, lengthy, fragile supply chain.
- Develop redundant manufacturing.
- Create strategic stockpiles (safety stock) of medications and raw materials.
- Invest in advanced manufacturing.

The FDA stated that they don't expect drug shortages for biotech medications. Do you want to know why? Biotech companies can afford and have implemented most of the initiatives above.

The solutions to drug shortages will not be easy and will take hard work, behavioral changes, and persistence. But the effort is worth the result. Our loved ones, friends, and colleagues depend on our success.

When I started Civica, I met a pediatric oncologist who told me how hard it is to inform parents that their child has cancer. He then said four generic drugs could cure 85% of childhood cancers. Then he asked to imagine telling a parent that the drug that will cure your child is in shortage and can't be acquired.

If this is not enough to boil your blood, our desire for cheap drugs has led to the globalization of the pharmaceutical supply chain to utilize companies like Intas from India. A December 2022 FDA Inspection of Intas questions our desire for cheap drugs.

As pharmaceutical professionals, we must say, "Enough is Enough," and demand that everyone who impacts the pharmaceutical supply chain change their approach. The organizations that must change include congressional leaders, policymakers, regulators and experts, pharmaceutical executives, purchasers, healthcare executives, healthcare providers, payors, insurers, and consumers. If we don't change, we don't have the right to complain about the results (shortages) of the system we have a part in creating.

Today, there is no way a single company can sustain itself selling an essential sterile injectable medication for less than two dollars!

The reasons I took on this challenge were multifaceted. I formulated, manufactured, or oversaw many of the drugs in shortage. I feel that the industry has failed, and I know that the government has no appetite to help the pharmaceutical industry, even to solve the shortage problem. However, I was also confident that we could gain support from health systems and supplies to decrease the number of shortages if we all worked together.

Chapter 29 - Country-Of-Origin Labeling

Country-of-origin labeling is a labeling requirement that indicates the country where a product was produced, manufactured, or grown. It is a legal requirement in some countries, including the United States, Canada, and the European Union, for certain products such as food, textiles, and automobiles. Country-of-origin labeling aims to inform consumers about the product's origin, enabling them to make informed purchasing decisions and support local economies. Country-of-origin labeling can also help ensure that products meet specific standards, such as environmental, safety, quality, or labor regulations, which vary by country.

Pharmaceuticals are not required to include country-of-origin labeling in the United States. When it states the manufacturer's name and address on a drug label, this does not necessarily mean the manufacturing location and could represent the location of the corporate headquarters. For example, Hospira's (a Pfizer Company) succinylcholine is not manufactured in Lake Forest, IL 60045, USA, since they do not have a commercial manufacturing site in Lake Forest.

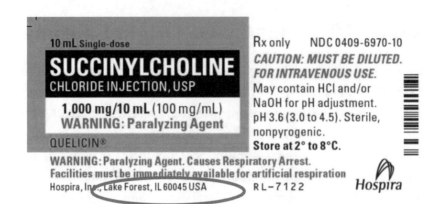

Someone will have to explain why I can know where my shirts and shoes are made but not my medications. This situation is the reverse of what most individuals would expect. I have advocated with Congressmen, Senators, their staff, FDA Officials, and others to add country-of-origin labeling to pharmaceuticals.

The FDA will state that they do not have the statutory authority to require Country of Origin Labeling. However, the FDA requires that all drugs, whether domestically or imported from abroad, meet the same safety, efficacy, and quality standards. However, not all foreign companies are ethical and intend to meet the FDA's expectations.

Pharmaceutical companies advocate that country-of-origin labeling is inappropriate for several reasons.

- One reason is that implementing labeling changes can be costly and time-consuming, especially for companies that manufacture drugs in multiple locations or use components from different countries.

170

- Another reason is that some companies may be concerned about the impact of country-of-origin labeling on their brand image or sales. For example, if a drug is manufactured in a country that is perceived as having lower quality standards, consumers may be less likely to trust the product and may choose a different brand.
- Additionally, some companies may be concerned about potential trade barriers or restrictions that could be imposed if country-of-origin labeling were required. This requirement could limit their ability to access certain markets or increase business costs.
- Pharma companies contend that where a product is made is a trade secret, and this knowledge provides valuable competitive intelligence.

I strongly assert that if a company is embarrassed about where a drug is produced, they should not manufacture a medication there, and I don't want to take that medication. Also, it is pure fiction that what country a drug is produced in provides a competitive advantage. It is also hard to justify that the additional cost burdens highly profitable branded pharmaceuticals. However, it is worth noting that many consumers and advocacy groups have called for more transparency and accountability in the pharmaceutical industry, including through country-of-origin labeling.

This information can help consumers make informed product decisions and promote greater supply chain accountability.

Dr. Erin Fox is a pharmacist and the senior director of drug information and support services at the University of Utah Health, and she has advocated for country-of-origin labeling in the pharmaceutical industry.

She has stated that country-of-origin labeling can provide valuable information to consumers about the safety and quality of the drugs they use. In addition, she has noted that some countries have lower quality standards for drug manufacturing and that consumers have a right to know where their drugs are coming from.

She has expressed that country-of-origin labeling, including the address of the manufacturing plant could help address drug shortages by promoting greater transparency and accountability in the pharmaceutical supply chain. By requiring companies to disclose the origin of their drugs, it would be easier to track and identify any issues or disruptions in the supply chain.

She has also noted that drug shortages often arise due to many factors, including manufacturing and quality control issues, regulatory hurdles, and pricing concerns. While country-of-origin labeling alone may not solve all of these issues, it could be a helpful tool for addressing some of the challenges related to supply chain disruptions.

Dr. Fox has argued that country-of-origin labeling can help promote transparency and accountability in the pharmaceutical supply chain. By requiring companies to disclose the origin of their drugs, consumers and regulators can better understand where potential safety, quality issues, or drug shortages may arise.

Chapter 30 - China's Stranglehold on the Drug Supply Chain

There are several concerns about drugs from China, including:

- Quality and safety: There have been counterfeit or substandard drugs from China entering the global market. These events raise concerns about the safety and effectiveness of these drugs. For example, several high-profile incidents involved substandard and counterfeit drugs from China, including adulterated heparin, cough syrup and melamine-tainted infant formula. These incidents led to numerous deaths and illnesses, highlighting the risks associated with drugs from China.

- Lack of regulatory oversight: Some critics argue that China's regulatory system for pharmaceuticals is not as rigorous as those in other countries, such as the United States or the European Union. This lack of regulatory oversight raises concerns about the quality and safety of drugs produced in China. For example, a 2018 report by the U.S.-China Economic and Security Review Commission found that China's pharmaceutical industry has a "suboptimal regulatory environment" and concerns about the safety and quality of drugs produced in China.

- Supply chain disruptions: The COVID-19 pandemic highlighted the vulnerability of the global pharmaceutical supply chain, which relies heavily on China to produce active pharmaceutical ingredients (APIs) and other key components. For example, India, which relies heavily on China for APIs, experienced significant disruptions to its pharmaceutical industry during the pandemic. Disruptions to this supply chain could lead to shortages of critical drugs. Approximately 3 of 4 essential medications do not have a United States source for the active ingredients.

- Political tensions: The ongoing political tensions between China and other countries, such as the United States, have raised concerns about the potential for China to use its control over the pharmaceutical supply chain as a bargaining chip in trade negotiations or other disputes. In fact, in 2020, there were reports that China was considering restricting the export of critical drugs and medical supplies during the COVID-19 pandemic. It has also been reported in the Chinese press that a high-ranking Chinese official threatened to suspend pharmaceutical exports to the United States as leverage when dealing with contested international affairs.

Overall, the concerns about drugs from China center around quality, safety, regulatory oversight, and supply chain vulnerabilities. Regulators and policymakers need to address these concerns to ensure the safety and availability of essential drugs for patients worldwide.

The following are some interesting stats:

- Generic medicines constitute nearly 86% of the drugs dispensed.[3]
- Of the 52 COVID-related medications, 75% have no U.S. source of the API (Active Pharmaceutical Ingredient) [1]
- Of the top 100 generic medicines consumed in the U.S., 83% had no U.S. source of the API [1]
- Of the 47 most prescribed antivirals, 97% had no U.S. source of API [1]
- Of the 111 most-prescribed antibiotics, 92% had no U.S. source of API
- 100% of Penicillins and 90% of Cephalosporins APIs come from China[2]
- Doxycycline: Only five Chinese manufacturers make doxycycline, and three were shut down, leading to drug shortages and a quadrupling in price. [3]
- Rifampin: A Chinese factory shut down, creating a worldwide shortage of the most effective TB treatment. [3]
- Hisun is the only manufacturer of several chemo drugs. The EU and USA prevented the import of Hisun drugs for approximately two years (2015-2017).[3]

1. https://olinblog.wustl.edu/2021/08/study-us-health-security-at-risk-because-of-medicine-manufacturing-limits/
2. https://timesofindia.indiatimes.com/business/india-business/china-supplies-over-80-of-pharma-raw-materials/articleshow/76453541.cms
3. ZEMBLA Documentary https://youtu.be/z6MtJSo_CAY

The United States is taking a multifaceted approach to address China's dominance in the pharmaceutical supply chain, focusing on reshoring, diversification, increased regulation, and managing intellectual property theft.

There has been a recent push to bring pharmaceutical manufacturing back to the United States. The government has provided funding and incentives for companies to build new facilities in the United States. It has also established partnerships with domestic manufacturers to ensure a stable supply of critical drugs.

Another approach has been diversifying the supply chain to reduce dependence on one country. This diversification includes increasing domestic manufacturing capabilities and establishing partnerships with other locations, such as Vietnam, South America, and Europe.

The United States government has also increased its regulatory oversight of drugs imported from China, focusing on ensuring the safety and quality of active pharmaceutical ingredients and other critical components. This oversight includes increased inspections and monitoring of Chinese facilities and efforts to improve information sharing and collaboration with Chinese regulators.

The United States government has also taken steps to address intellectual property theft by Chinese companies, particularly concerning the theft of trade secrets and proprietary technology related to drug development and manufacturing.

I know Congress and the White House are actively investigating other approaches to reduce our dependency on China, and it will be interesting to follow future developments.

Civica has successfully sourced sterile injectable drugs using non-Chinese sourced API from American, European, and Japanese suppliers. However, this comes at a small cost premium, which is passed onto our members.

Chapter 31 - Risk of Counterfeit Drugs is Growing, & is Global

Counterfeit, adulterated, and substandard drugs, especially the 2007 -2008 adulterated heparin situation I described earlier in the book, moved me to create Rx-360.

Counterfeit drugs are a global problem and have been uncovered in the U.S., Europe, and developing countries. The WHO estimates that up to 30% of drugs sold in developing countries are counterfeit. In some African countries, this figure could be 90%. Counterfeit drugs can include fake versions of patented drugs and fake versions of generic drugs. Counterfeit drugs can be dangerous as they may contain the wrong active ingredient, the incorrect amount of active ingredient, or even harmful substances.

Source: sitbosystems

181

In addition to the danger to public health, counterfeit drugs have a significant economic impact. The WHO estimates that the global cost of counterfeit drugs is billions of dollars annually. This cost includes the cost of treating patients whom counterfeit drugs have harmed.

The WHO and other organizations have been working to address the issue by strengthening regulation and law enforcement, improving supply chain security, and raising awareness among healthcare professionals and the public.

The prevalence of counterfeit drugs in Africa, where the problem is the worst, can be attributed to several factors, including weak regulatory systems, lack of infrastructure for drug testing and distribution, and extreme poverty levels. In addition, many African countries have a high demand for medicines, which can make them a target for counterfeiters looking to profit from the sale of fake drugs.

Counterfeit drugs can be dangerous or even deadly. They often contain the wrong active ingredient or no active agreement, which can cause serious health problems or even death. In addition, counterfeit drugs can also contribute to the development of drug resistance, making it harder to treat diseases in the future.

Counterfeit drugs are a significant public health concern. They can undermine trust in the healthcare system, discourage individuals from seeking medical care, and contribute to the spread of drug-resistant infections. They also have a significant economic impact, undermining the legitimate pharmaceutical industry and draining resources from healthcare systems.

There are examples of counterfeit drugs globally. Examples include:

- Antimalarials: Counterfeit antimalarials, used to treat malaria, have been found in many parts of Africa. These fake drugs may contain no active ingredient or the wrong active ingredient, making them ineffective against the disease.
- Weight loss medication: In 2014, the FDA warned consumers about counterfeit versions of the weight loss medication Alli® that were being sold online. The counterfeit versions contained a different active ingredient than the legitimate medication, which could cause serious side effects. In 2023, The FDA and Novo Nordisk reported that a counterfeit semaglutide injection (Ozempic) pen was found in the United States.
- Erectile dysfunction medication: Counterfeit versions of erectile dysfunction medications such as Viagra® and Cialis® have been found in the United States. These counterfeit versions may contain harmful ingredients, or they may contain no active ingredient at all.
- Antibiotics: In 2015, the FDA warned healthcare providers about counterfeit versions of the antibiotic Bactrim® being sold in the United States. The counterfeit versions contained only a fraction of the active ingredient in the legitimate medication, which could lead to treatment failure and the development of antibiotic-resistant infections.

- Pain medication: Counterfeit versions of pain medications such as OxyContin® and Vicodin® have been discovered in the United States. These counterfeit versions may contain dangerous substances, such as fentanyl, which can cause serious harm or death.

It is important to note that these are just a few examples, and the list of counterfeit drugs can be much longer and different based on distinct locations.

It is impossible to prevent criminals from counterfeiting. Therefore, the task is to detect counterfeits as quickly as possible, remove counterfeit drugs from the market, and punish the counterfeiters.

Drugs that are susceptible to counterfeiting should have counterfeit-detecting technologies built into the product. For example, drugs and their packaging should contain Overt, Covert, and Forensic measures for detection.

Overt: A type of security measure that's visible to the naked eye so that it can be detected without any tools, such as a hologram and tampered evident seals

Covert: Secret protection that's undetectable unless you know it's there, such as security inks and other tags that require detection with unique readers. This information is provided to law enforcement and customs operations.

Forensic: Only a few individuals within the company know what forensic techniques are used. Investigation services can use that information to trace where a breach in security happened and how to prevent it in the future.

The amount of counterfeit drugs is significantly unreported and undetected. What is found and reported is just the tip of the iceberg. The following figure demonstrates this fact.

The Problem is Larger Than We Know

Threat	Detected
Viagra	Minimal
Inferior API causing shortages	100s
Lethal impurities in Emerging Markets	1,000s
Substandard products globally	10,000s
Poorly formulated medicines and fake medicines in Africa	100,000s

Source: Roger Bate, AEI, Washington, D.C.

Examples of counterfeit drugs have been discovered in the United States and Europe. One example is the case of a fake cancer drug that was found to be distributed in the US and Europe in 2012 and 2015. The drug Avastin®, a cancer drug, was found to contain no active ingredient. Another example is the case of counterfeit Lipitor®, a cholesterol-lowering medication, which was found to be distributed in the US in 2011. The fake Lipitor® pills were found to contain talcum powder instead of the active ingredient.

In 2020, the U.S. FDA reported a spike in the number of counterfeit drugs entering the U.S. market, including COVID-19 treatment drugs, which puts American lives at risk.

Another example is in 2020, Italian police seized a large batch of counterfeit drugs worth around €20m ($22m). The haul included more than one million tablets and capsules, including fakes of the anti-inflammatory drug diclofenac and the anti-anxiety medication alprazolam. Additionally, in 2021, The EMA (European Medicines Agency) issued a warning about the circulation of counterfeit versions of the COVID-19 vaccine. These examples demonstrate that the problem of counterfeit drugs is a global issue, and it is important for authorities to remain vigilant in their efforts to detect and remove these dangerous products from the market.

There are examples of counterfeit drugs in Asia, including:

- In India, fake versions of popular drugs such as anti-cancer drugs, antibiotics, and anti-retroviral drugs have been found on the market. Sometimes, these fake drugs contain harmful ingredients.
- In China, counterfeit versions of drugs such as Viagra®, Lipitor®, and other popular drugs have been found in the market.
- In Indonesia, fake versions of malaria drugs have been found on the market, which can lead to treatment failure and drug resistance.
- In the Philippines, counterfeit drugs such as antibiotics, painkillers, and anti-inflammatory drugs have been found on the market.
- In Vietnam, fake versions of antibiotics and anti-inflammatory drugs have been found on the market.

In China, there have been instances of counterfeit drugs being sold in the market. In recent years, fake cancer drugs have been a significant problem. In 2018, it was reported that a fake version of a cancer drug called Avastin was being sold to patients. The counterfeit drug contained no active ingredient and contained salt water and other cheap ingredients. In another case, a fake version of a drug called Erbitux® used to treat colon cancer was found to have been distributed across China. The counterfeit version contained no active ingredient and was made of starch and other cheap ingredients.

These examples show the serious risks that counterfeit drugs pose to public health, as they may not provide any therapeutic benefit to patients and could even cause harm.

There have been examples of counterfeit drugs in South America. For instance, counterfeit drugs such as Viagra®, Lipitor®, and Tamiflu® have been found in Brazil. In Colombia, fake versions of drugs such as antibiotics and anti-inflammatory medications have been reported. In Peru, counterfeit drugs for hypertension and diabetes have been discovered. These counterfeit drugs may contain the wrong active ingredients, too little or too much active ingredients, or impurities that can harm patients. These examples highlight the importance of stringent regulations and effective enforcement to combat the production and distribution of counterfeit drugs in South America and worldwide.

Professional and trade organizations are working to detect and prevent counterfeit drugs. Here are examples:

- The National Association of Boards of Pharmacy (NABP): The NABP is an organization that represents the state boards of pharmacy in the United States. The organization works to protect public health by verifying the legitimacy of online pharmacies, promoting the use of prescription drug monitoring programs, and providing resources for healthcare providers to help prevent the introduction of counterfeit drugs into the supply chain.

- The Pharmaceutical Security Institute (PSI): The PSI is a trade organization that works to protect the pharmaceutical supply chain from counterfeit drugs and other threats. The organization provides training and resources to pharmaceutical companies, regulatory agencies, and law enforcement agencies to help them prevent and respond to incidents of counterfeiting.

- The Healthcare Distribution Alliance (HDA): The HDA is a trade organization representing the pharmaceutical distribution industry in the United States. The organization works to ensure the safety and security of the pharmaceutical supply chain by promoting the use of track-and-trace systems, conducting training and education programs, and collaborating with regulatory agencies, law enforcement, and other stakeholders to prevent the introduction of counterfeit drugs into the supply chain.

- The International Pharmaceutical Federation (FIP): The FIP is a global organization representing pharmacists and pharmaceutical scientists. The organization promotes the safe and effective use of medication by raising awareness about the risks of counterfeit drugs, promoting anti-counterfeiting technologies, and providing resources for pharmacists to help detect and prevent counterfeit drugs.

- Rx-360 has various initiatives to detect and prevent counterfeit drugs, including a program to verify the authenticity of pharmaceutical ingredients and a program to promote the use of track-and-trace systems. The organization also promotes supply chain transparency by encouraging companies to disclose information about their suppliers and supply chain practices.

These organizations, among others, work to promote the safety and effectiveness of medication by detecting and preventing counterfeit drugs from entering the supply chain.

Consumers can take steps to protect themselves from counterfeit drugs and other supply chain risks. Here are a few tips:

- Purchase medication from a reputable source: Only purchase medication from a licensed pharmacy or healthcare provider. Be wary of purchasing medicines from unverified online sources or from individuals selling drugs on the street.
- Verify the authenticity of medication: Check the medication's packaging, labeling, and appearance to ensure it matches what you are used to seeing. Be suspicious of medication that appears to be tampered with or has unusual packaging or labeling.
- Report suspected counterfeit medication: If you suspect you have received it, report it to the appropriate authorities, such as the FDA or your state board of pharmacy.

- Be aware of potential supply chain risks: Stay informed about the dangers of counterfeit drugs and other supply chain issues by reading reputable sources of information, such as the FDA's website or news articles from trusted sources.
- Work with healthcare providers: Consult with your healthcare provider if you have any concerns about the safety or effectiveness of your medication. They can provide guidance and advice on how to stay safe and avoid counterfeit drugs.

Overall, consumers can actively protect themselves from counterfeit drugs and other supply chain risks by being vigilant, informed, and working with healthcare providers.

Chapter 32 - Supply Chain Problems That Kill

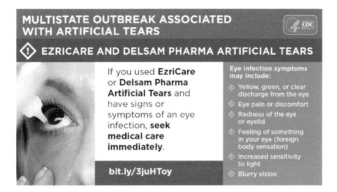

Eye Drops:

A Centers for Disease Control and Prevention report now says the drops are linked to nearly seventy sickened patients in 16 states.

According to reports, at least six individuals died due to the contamination, and hundreds suffered from eye infections and other complications.

In addition to the fatalities, eight individuals have reported permanent vision loss, and four others lost an eye. Officials say a rare strain of drug-resistant bacteria, Pseudomonas aeruginosa, is to blame. The bacterium had never been found in the U.S. before the outbreak.

There have been several other incidents involving contaminated eye drops in the past that have resulted in fatalities. One example is the 2011 case of contaminated eye drops produced by a pharmaceutical company in China. The company had used an unapproved ingredient in its eye drops, which resulted in a bacterial infection that caused severe damage to the eyes of patients who used the drops.

In addition, the incident led to widespread recalls of the contaminated eye drops and investigations into the safety and quality of pharmaceutical products produced in China.

These incidents highlight the risks associated with a global pharmaceutical supply chain, particularly when ensuring the safety and quality of drugs and medical products. It also underscores the importance of regulatory oversight and enforcement and the need for greater transparency and accountability in the pharmaceutical industry.

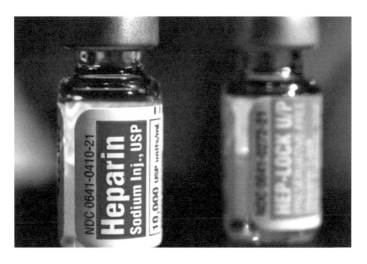

Heparin:

These deaths were later traced back to the adulteration of heparin with a cheaper substance called oversulfated chondroitin sulfate (OSCS).

The adulteration of heparin with OSCS was a deliberate act of economically motivated fraud, likely carried out by suppliers in China. OSCS is a similar-looking substance to heparin but has a different chemical structure and can cause severe allergic reactions in some patients.

The adulterated heparin caused various adverse reactions, including difficulty breathing, nausea, vomiting, low blood pressure, and even death. When the contaminated heparin was introduced into the US market, the contamination resulted in 246 deaths and hundreds of serious injuries, leading to a significant global health crisis.

Since then, the FDA and other regulatory agencies worldwide have continued to monitor heparin products closely to prevent similar adulteration incidents. These efforts include enhanced testing and analysis methods, increased oversight of the supply chain, and improved communication and coordination between regulatory agencies and manufacturers.

The incident highlighted the risks associated with relying on a limited number of suppliers and the need for greater oversight and regulation of the pharmaceutical supply chain. It also underscored the importance of transparency and accountability in the industry, as well as the need for rigorous testing and quality control measures to ensure the safety and efficacy of drugs.

From April 30, 2008, New York Times article by Gardiner Harris.

"LeRoy Hubley of Toledo, Ohio, described how both his 65-year-old wife and his 47-year-old son died within a few weeks of each other. Both suffered from a genetic kidney disease that required constant dialysis, for which heparin is routinely used.

"As Christmas music softly played in the background, we each said our goodbyes," Mr. Hubley said, breaking down in tears. "Then my wife and love of 48 years drifted away."

For weeks after their deaths, he did not know that his wife, Bonnie, and son, Randy, had been given contaminated heparin.

"Now I am left to deal not only with the pain of losing my wife and son but anger that an unsafe drug was permitted to be sold in this country," he said.

Avastin:

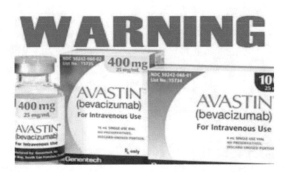

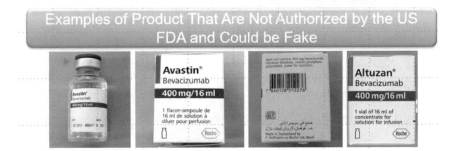

The counterfeit versions of the drug contained no active ingredient and posed a serious risk to patients.

Unlike Avastin, produced by Roche, the counterfeit medication did not contain the active ingredient Bevacizumab, resulting in ineffective treatment for cancer patients. In addition, other dangerous foreign ingredients were used in the formulation.

The involved oncologists were not sourcing the drug from legitimate United States suppliers for price reasons. At the time, a 400mg dose of the medication cost around $2,000. Depending on the illness, the cost for a treatment cycle can run from $65,000 to $110,000.

The growing globalized trade in parallel imports means that medication – including the real thing – is sometimes more cheaply available when procured through less transparent channels.

Complex & Insecure Supply Chain Leads to Counterfeit Avastin in US After Taking a Global Route

6. US Oncologist
- Orders solicited by Montana Healthcare Solutions at $400 below market value. Montana Healthcare is a licensed Wholesaler in Montana
- When an orders is placed it is with a different company in Barbados
- Product Shipped from Volunteer Distribution
- FDA Issues safety alert

5. Britain
- Quality Specialty Products (QSP) aka Montana Health Care Solutions, a known pharmaceutical diverter
- Authorities confiscated majority of the counterfeit product
- Some counterfeit product was sent to the US Oncologist before being confiscated
- 36 vials still missing

4. Caremed of Denmark
- Received order from Hadicon
- Sent counterfeit product to Britain

3. Hadicon of Switzerland
- Trades in pharmaceuticals via parallel trade
- Licensed by Swissmedic
- Switzerland is the only country that grants permission to trade in pharmaceuticals outside its borders
- There are 60 such Swiss companies

1. Istanbul, Turkey
- SAWA obtained the counterfeit Avastin from a Syrian middleman who acquired it from Turkey
- Product was counterfeit with no active ingredient
- Product contained salt, starch, acetone and other chemicals

2. SAWA in Egypt
- Conducted no testing of the product
- Filled the order for Hadicon
- SAWA not licensed by Egyptian MOH to import or export drugs

From My 2014 United States Senate H.E.L.P Committee Testimony

Hadicon ordered the medication in Egypt from a company called SAWA for importing and exporting, then stored the goods in a Zurich duty-free warehouse before sending them to Caremed in Denmark.

Hadicon conducts trading in pharmaceuticals via parallel trade licensed by Swissmedic. Switzerland is the only country that grants permission to parallel trade in pharmaceuticals outside its borders. There are sixty such Swiss companies.

SAWA obtained the counterfeit Avastin from a Syrian middleman who acquired it from Turkey. The product was counterfeit with no active Ingredient and contained salt, starch, acetone, and other chemicals. Roche confirmed through testing that there was no Bevacizumab present.

The Danish intermediary sent the order to Britain, from where it was dispatched to the US.

Quality Specialty Products (QSP), aka Montana Health Care Solutions, is a known pharmaceutical diverter in Britain. Authorities confiscated the majority of the counterfeit drugs. However, some fake drugs were sent to the US Oncologist before being confiscated.

The oncologist ordered the counterfeit Avastin from Montana Health Care through Barbados. Two of these oncologists were in Thousand Oaks, California, where my family lived at the time, and most likely, I knew some patients whom these oncologists treated!

Glycerin:

The first instance of contaminated cough syrup that gained significant attention was the 1937 Elixir Sulfanilamide tragedy in the United States. The medication contained diethylene glycol, a toxic substance commonly used as a solvent, which led to the deaths of more than 100 people. This event prompted the U.S. Congress to pass the Federal Food, Drug, and Cosmetic Act in 1938, establishing stricter drug safety and testing regulations.

More than 80 years later, the same events continue to happen; however, recent events are intentional adulterations for economic gains.

Let me give you an example where a lack of transparency in the supply chain could be exploited, as demonstrated in the map I submitted to the United States Senate H.E.L.P Committee. The data for the supply chain map was provided in the National Geographic video "Illicit: The Dark Trade."

Glycerin is an inactive ingredient used in many pharmaceuticals. In this case, the government of Panama unknowingly purchased adulterated glycerin to be used in cough syrup, which resulted in at least sixty-seven deaths. The investigation into this tragedy revealed several supply chain breakdowns hidden from the manufacturer purchasing the ingredient.

As illustrated in the map, the problem began in China at the Taixing glycerin factory, which produced a technical substitute for glycerin, which was not pure glycerin but contained antifreeze. Antifreeze is three times cheaper than glycerin. The Chinese FDA never inspected the Taixing glycerin factory. As boxes 2, 3, and 4 on the chart describe how a series of brokers and traders moved the material through the supply chain, changing the name of the material, the manufacturing site, and the product's expiration date and performing no testing. This adulterated glycerin was used to manufacture cough medicine, leading to fatal consequences.

Learning from this example, if anyone in the supply chain, including the cough syrup manufacturer, tested the glycerin, they would know they were purchasing antifreeze. As a result, these fatalities could have been prevented, which is why transparency in the supply chain is so important.

Update: During the writing of this book, another example of adulterating cough syrup with cheap antifreeze, which is a criminal action, has occurred. The WHO reported the deaths of more than 300 infants on three continents, and more should be expected over the next several years because undetected adulterated barrels remain in warehouses.

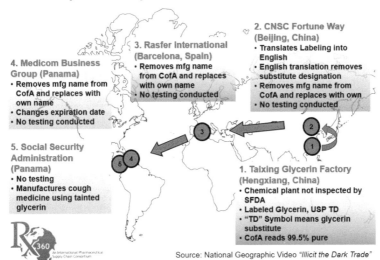

Complex & Insecure Supply Chains Lead to Tragic Consequences: Glycerin > 100 Panamanian Deaths

2. CNSC Fortune Way (Beijing, China)
- Translates Labeling into English
- English translation removes substitute designation
- Removes mfg name from CofA and replaces with own
- No testing conducted

3. Rasfer International (Barcelona, Spain)
- Removes mfg name from CofA and replaces with own name
- No testing conducted

4. Medicom Business Group (Panama)
- Removes mfg name from CofA and replaces with own name
- Changes expiration date
- No testing conducted

5. Social Security Administration (Panama)
- No testing
- Manufactures cough medicine using tainted glycerin

1. Taixing Glycerin Factory (Hengxiang, China)
- Chemical plant not inspected by SFDA
- Labeled Glycerin, USP TD
- "TD" Symbol means glycerin substitute
- CofA reads 99.5% pure

Source: National Geographic Video *"Illicit the Dark Trade"*

From My 2014 United State Senate H.E.L.P Committee Testimony

Chapter 33 - Without Trust: There is No Pharma Industry

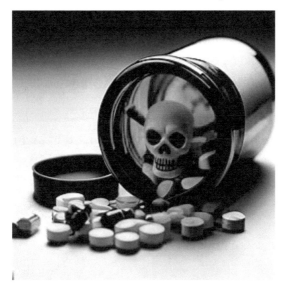

Regulators, healthcare providers, patients, and consumers can never watch how clinical studies or manufacturing occurs within the pharmaceutical industry. So, our stakeholders depend on a "trust but verify" system led by the Quality Unit and the FDA.

"Trust takes years to build, seconds to break, and forever to repair."

This paradigm is particularly true in the pharmaceutical industry, where trust is critical for ensuring the safety and efficacy of medications.

Pharmaceutical companies are, first and foremost, data companies. Pharmaceutical companies are often called data companies because they generate and analyze vast amounts of data throughout drug development. They must document almost every aspect of manufacturing, including testing raw materials through finished products. Neither the FDA nor the patient is in the room when every batch is produced. The system is based on a "trust and verify" approach.

Pharmaceutical companies must work hard to build and maintain trust with regulatory agencies, healthcare providers, patients, and consumers. This effort includes being transparent about their research and development processes, ensuring the quality and reliability of their data, and being responsive to concerns and feedback from stakeholders.

When you consume that tiny white tablet, you do so based on trust that everyone did their job correctly.

However, a single incident of data manipulation, fraudulent behavior, or other violations of trust can quickly erode that trust and have severe consequences for the company and its stakeholders. These destructive behaviors can lead to regulatory sanctions, legal action, and damage to a company's reputation.

Therefore, it is essential to prioritize data integrity and ethical behavior in all aspects of the business to build and maintain trust with stakeholders. This work includes investing in robust quality management systems, promoting a culture of ethical behavior and transparency, and proactively addressing any concerns or issues. By doing so, pharmaceutical companies can help ensure their drugs are safe and effective and maintain their stakeholders' trust.

The pharmaceutical industry increasingly relies on data to drive its research, development, manufacturing, quality, and marketing efforts. In fact, a pharma company can be considered a data company for several reasons.

Firstly, pharma companies collect vast amounts of data through clinical trials, real-world studies, and other research initiatives. This data includes everything from patient demographics and medical history to treatment outcomes and adverse events. By analyzing this data, pharma companies can gain insights into their drugs' safety and efficacy, identify improvement areas, and make informed decisions about their drug development pipelines.

Secondly, pharma companies use data to inform their marketing strategies. For example, they analyze market trends, physician prescribing patterns, and patient preferences to identify target audiences and develop targeted marketing campaigns. They also use data to track the effectiveness of their marketing efforts and adjust their strategies accordingly.

Thirdly, pharma companies use data to optimize their manufacturing processes. They analyze production data to identify inefficiencies and implement process improvements to increase productivity and reduce costs.

Lastly, pharma companies use data to comply with regulatory requirements. They must collect and submit data to regulatory agencies to gain drug approval and maintain compliance with ongoing regulatory requirements.

In summary, pharma companies are increasingly relying on data to drive their research, development, and marketing efforts, as well as to optimize their manufacturing processes and comply with regulatory requirements. With the increasing importance of data in the pharmaceutical industry, it is not surprising that pharma companies are seen as data companies.

Therefore, data integrity is critical in the pharmaceutical industry. It is fundamental to ensuring pharmaceutical drug safety, efficacy, and quality.

Data integrity refers to data's completeness, accuracy, and consistency throughout its entire lifecycle. It is essential because decisions based on inaccurate or incomplete data can lead to severe consequences, such as approving unsafe or ineffective drugs or rejecting safe and effective drugs.

The pharmaceutical industry is highly regulated, and regulatory agencies require that companies maintain high data integrity standards. These requirements include ensuring data is appropriately recorded, stored, and maintained throughout the product lifecycle. Companies must also have effective quality management systems to ensure that data is complete, accurate, and dependable.

Pharmaceutical companies are responsible for generating data from clinical trials, real-world studies, and other research initiatives to demonstrate the safety and efficacy of their drugs. This data is then submitted to regulatory agencies like the FDA for review and approval.

The FDA has rigorous data quality standards, and companies must demonstrate that their data is complete, accurate, and dependable.

The FDA also reviews the data to ensure the medication is safe and effective for its intended use.

Data integrity is also critical in pharma manufacturing. It is just as important in manufacturing as in clinical trials and research.

Pharmaceutical manufacturing involves the production of medications, which includes the formulation, testing, and packaging of drugs. This process generates essential data that must be recorded and maintained to ensure the medication is safe and effective.

For example, companies must ensure that the right ingredients are used in the correct amounts and that the manufacturing process is performed according to established procedures. Then, Quality Control evaluates each batch to verify that the process was followed and that the drug meets specifications. This data must be accurately recorded and maintained to ensure the medication is produced consistently and meets the required quality standards.

Regulatory agencies like the FDA require that pharmaceutical companies maintain high data integrity standards during R&D in their clinical studies and manufacturing processes. These requirements include ensuring that data is recorded accurately and completely, stored securely and that manufacturing processes are validated and controlled. Data integrity is vital to the FDA since they are not present when the data is generated, leaving no other option for the FDA but to "trust but verify" through strict enforcement of data integrity requirements and periodic inspections.

Any data integrity violations can have profound consequences, such as producing unsafe or ineffective medications, regulatory sanctions, and damage to a company's reputation.

Therefore, pharmaceutical companies must maintain high data integrity standards throughout the manufacturing process to ensure the safety and efficacy of medications.

The pharmaceutical industry's future depends on maintaining the trust of regulatory agencies, healthcare providers, patients, and consumers. When anyone opens their medicine container and looks at a little white tablet, they cannot determine if the medication is safe and effective. Yet, the doctor prescribes the medication, a healthcare provider dispenses and sometimes administers the drug, and the patient consumes the medicine, all based on trust. An industry-wide breaking of that trust would be a disaster to the industry, causing unforeseen consequences to employees, health systems, health care providers, and patients.

Overall, the pharmaceutical industry relies on data integrity to ensure the safety and efficacy of medications. Likewise, patients, healthcare providers, and regulatory agencies like the FDA must trust the data generated by pharmaceutical companies to make informed decisions about the medicines they prescribe and use.

For these reasons, any data integrity violations are considered a major violation, and the FDA will take severe enforcement actions, which could include debarment to incarceration.

Chapter 34 - When Shit Happens

"When shit happens" means that unexpected and unfortunate events occur. It is a way of acknowledging that sometimes things do not go as planned and accepting that there will be setbacks and challenges. When "shit happens," it is essential to stay calm, assess the situation, and take appropriate action to mitigate the damage or find a solution. Learning from that experience and using it as an opportunity for growth and improvement is also essential.

Making drugs is difficult and complex and does depend on individuals doing the right thing to be successful. No matter how good an operation is within a company, stuff goes wrong. How a company handles these events determines if the company is sub-par, good, or great. I have had the opportunity to work for and with each type of those companies.

Sub-par companies put their head in the sand, ignore the events leading up to additional significant failures, and some may even try to hide the adverse events.

Great companies are proactive, encourage and communicate the prompt reporting of near misses, eliminate the fear of reporting events, conduct management reviews, take a no-stone-unturned approach to find root causes, and implement corrective actions.

One thing that used to drive me crazy was that something would go sideways on a Monday. The individuals involved would not ask for help, would try to resolve the event, and as things worsened, they panicked. Finally, on a Friday, just before the end of the day, I would get a phone call to dump the problem in my lap. I learned that when this happened, the individuals reporting the event got the problem off their chests and could enjoy the weekend. Individuals who demonstrate this behavior should understand that it is not appreciated and is career-limiting.

This behavior would even happen at great companies where the importance of prompt reporting was not clearly communicated.

Individuals need to recognize that asking for help is not a weakness. Addressing problems promptly is paramount in both personal and professional spheres, as it can significantly impact outcomes and overall well-being.

Swiftly tackling challenges allows us to prevent issues from escalating, saving time, resources, and emotional energy in the long run. When problems are promptly addressed, they are still manageable, and potential negative consequences can be minimized or avoided altogether.

As a younger executive, I would accept their baggage. As I got older and wiser, I counseled these individuals that they still owned the problem and that their behavior was not good for their careers.

Chapter 35 - Revolutionizing Pharmaceutical Manufacturing:

The Implementation of Artificial Intelligence in the Factory

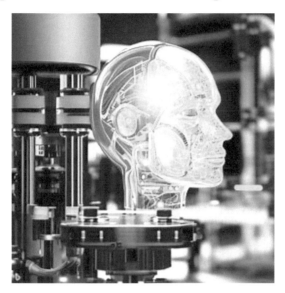

Manufacturing has always been at the forefront of technological innovation. However, with the advent of Artificial Intelligence (AI), it has an unprecedented opportunity to transform its operations and revolutionize the industry. Implementing AI can help manufacturers achieve greater efficiency, reduce costs, and improve quality control. The potential benefits of AI in manufacturing are too significant to ignore.

Isn't it just amazing how Artificial Intelligence is finding its way into pharmaceutical manufacturing? There's this incredible potential for AI to make everything run smoother and more efficiently in the industry, and I can't help but be hopeful about what's to come. Let me break down some of the most exciting points about AI in pharmaceutical manufacturing:

Quality Control and Assurance: It's like having a super sharp-eyed helper who can spot even the tiniest defects in medicines and packaging. We're talking about a serious boost in accuracy for quality checks with AI.

Process Optimization: Imagine if AI were our guide to finding the best paths through a maze of data. It's like having a compass that points us to more efficient ways of making medicines, reducing waste, and maximizing our resources.

Predictive Maintenance: AI seems like the psychic of machinery, foretelling when things might go wrong. This means fewer unexpected hiccups and smoother sailing through production.

Supply Chain Management: AI is like a crystal ball that predicts what medicines will be needed, when they're needed, and ensures they're always in stock. No more waiting around or running out of essential medications.

Regulatory Compliance: AI is like a rulebook that never closes, ensuring everything is up to code. It's like having a guardian angel to keep everything on the right track.

Data Analysis: AI is like a detective that uncovers hidden secrets in complex data. It's like having a sixth sense for spotting potential issues that might go unnoticed.

Automation: AI-powered robots? That's like having an army of tireless workers who don't get tired or make mistakes. It's all about smoother operations and fewer errors.

Real-time Monitoring: Imagine having a watchful eye that never blinks during the manufacturing process. AI makes that possible, ensuring the quality is maintained without any slips.

Risk Assessment: AI is like a wizard with a magic crystal ball that can predict potential risks. It helps us take preventive measures before things even have a chance to go wrong.

Drug Formulation: Think of AI as an expert chef crafting the perfect recipe. It's all about designing drugs that are stable, soluble, and effective, tailored for the best possible outcomes.

While we're stepping into this AI wonderland in pharmaceutical manufacturing, we've got to be cautious too. It's like walking on new terrain – we must consider data security, ethics, and other essential factors. But the future looks so bright! Researchers and professionals are like explorers, charting new paths to maximize AI's potential in this field. Just thinking about all the possibilities fills me with excitement and hope!

There are key technologies that enable artificial intelligence, including:

1. Augmented Reality and Smart Glasses
2. Machine Learning
3. Natural Language Processing
4. Computer Vision
5. Robotics
6. Big data Analytics
7. Internet of Things (IoT)
8. Quality 4.0

These technologies work together to enable artificial intelligence, allowing computer systems to perform tasks that typically require human intelligence and improve outcomes in various applications.

Augmented Reality, Virtual Reality, and Smart Glasses

The pharmaceutical industry benefits from technology and innovation, with new tools and technologies that have helped improve manufacturing processes, drug development, and quality control procedures. The popular technologies that have recently emerged include Augmented Reality (AR), Virtual Reality (VR), and smart glasses. These technologies can improve efficiency, accuracy, and safety, transforming the pharmaceutical industry. This essay examines the pharmaceutical industry's use of virtual reality and smart glasses, including their costs, benefits, and pitfalls.

Augmented Reality (AR) in Pharmaceutical Research and Development (R&D), Manufacturing, and Quality Control have several benefits. AR can create 3D models of molecules and proteins, enabling researchers to visualize and interact with them more effectively, accelerating the drug discovery and development process. Additionally, AR technology can improve manufacturing and quality control by providing workers with real-time data and information. AR can identify potential defects or issues, allowing workers to address them before they become significant problems, and simulate manufacturing processes for workers to practice their skills in a safe environment.

Better Patient Education and Engagement can also be improved using AR technology in the pharmaceutical industry. For example, AR can provide visual aids and instructions to help patients properly take medication, reducing the risk of medication errors and product complaints. AR can also inform patients about their condition and treatment options, improving patient education and engagement.

Virtual Reality (VR) in Pharmaceutical Manufacturing and Quality Control can simulate and visualize manufacturing processes and quality control procedures. It can simulate drug interactions and visualize the molecular structure of drugs, providing an immersive experience for researchers and allowing them to design better drugs. VR can also simulate the mixing and blending of active ingredients to ensure that the final product has the desired properties. Additionally, VR technology can help quality control professionals detect defects in the production process and identify potential sources of contamination.

Smart Glasses in Pharmaceutical Manufacturing and Quality Control can improve efficiency and effectiveness in various processes. For example, smart glasses can provide workers with real-time data and information, allowing them to make better decisions and perform tasks more efficiently. It can also enhance worker safety, training, and productivity. These visual aids can also help operators to complete assignments correctly.

Although implementing augmented reality, virtual reality, and smart glasses in the pharmaceutical industry can be costly, the benefits of improved worker safety, enhanced training, and improved productivity can lead to improved patient outcomes and profitability.

Machine Learning

Machine learning is becoming increasingly important in pharmaceutical manufacturing because it helps to make production processes more efficient and effective. This advancement means that by using machine learning, we can use computer programs and mathematical models to analyze data from various stages of the manufacturing process. We can then use this information to identify patterns and insights that can help us improve production.

Process optimization is one of the most promising machine-learning applications in pharmaceutical manufacturing. Machine learning algorithms can identify factors that impact product quality and production efficiency by analyzing data from various stages of the manufacturing process, such as raw materials and equipment performance. This information can then be used to optimize production processes, reduce waste, and improve product quality.

Machine learning can also help us improve product quality by identifying defects early in manufacturing. By analyzing data from quality control inspections and process monitoring sensors, machine learning algorithms can identify patterns that indicate potential defects before they happen. Identifying patterns allows us to take corrective action during manufacturing, preventing costly investigations and batch rejections.

Another way machine learning can be used in pharmaceutical manufacturing is through predictive maintenance. By analyzing data from equipment sensors and maintenance logs, machine learning algorithms can identify patterns that indicate potential equipment failures before they occur. Identifying patterns allows us to schedule maintenance proactively, reducing downtime and improving equipment reliability.

In fact, using machine learning can help manufacturing processes achieve a 6 Sigma plus performance, which means a failure rate of only 3.4 defects per million opportunities. It's common to see machine learning manufacturing processes perform at 20+ Sigma, which translates to a failure rate of "once in a blue moon" or only one defect in 3.4 billion attempts for a 20 Sigma performing process. Providing this reliability data to regulatory agencies like the FDA, they are more likely to be open to applications to eliminate in-process testing and even finished product testing.

For those who are skeptics, I have had organizations measure and improve processes, then continuously monitor the process, developing reliability data and making submissions to regulators globally to eliminate specifications where the risk of failure was "once in a blue moon" for numerous products at several companies.

Overall, machine learning has the potential to improve the efficiency and effectiveness of pharmaceutical manufacturing significantly. As technology evolves, we will see more widespread adoption of machine learning in the industry.

Natural Language Processing

Natural language processing (NLP) is a branch of artificial intelligence focusing on the interaction between computers and human language. The ultimate goal of NLP is to teach computers to understand, interpret, and generate human language in a way similar to how humans communicate.

In the pharmaceutical manufacturing industry, NLP can be used to analyze and understand large volumes of text-based data. This methodology includes data from scientific literature, regulatory documents, product complaint files, deviation and non-conformance reports, logbooks, and more. As a result, NLP benefits drug discovery and development and ensures compliance with regulatory requirements.

By enabling faster and more accurate analysis of text-based data, NLP can help drive innovation, improve safety, and support regulatory compliance in pharmaceutical manufacturing. In addition, NLP is a powerful tool that can help make sense of the enormous amounts of data generated in the industry, ultimately leading to better products and processes.

Computer Vision

Computer vision is a type of artificial intelligence that helps computers understand and analyze visual information, such as images or videos. This methodology uses complex mathematical models that allow the computer to identify and classify objects, patterns, and images.

In the pharmaceutical industry, computer vision can be applied in many ways, including quality control, inspection, and monitoring of manufacturing processes. For example, it can inspect pharmaceutical products for defects that do not meet quality standards, like scratches, cracks, or discolorations.

Additionally, computer vision can monitor manufacturing processes in real-time to detect anomalies or deviations from expected behavior, such as clogs or blockages. It can also track products moving through the production process, from raw materials to finished products, ensuring they are correctly labeled and packaged.

Computer vision can significantly improve pharmaceutical manufacturing efficiency, safety, and quality by providing faster and more accurate visual data analysis. It's a powerful tool that can help ensure that products meet the highest quality and safety standards.

Robotics

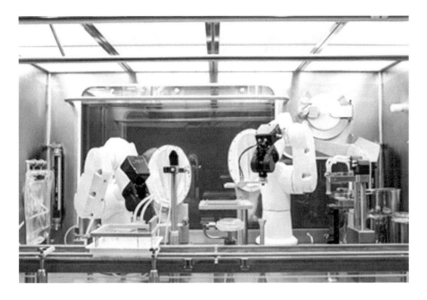

In simple terms, robotics is the field of designing, developing, and deploying robots that can perform tasks independently or with minimal human intervention. In the pharmaceutical manufacturing industry, robotics can be used in numerous ways, such as:

Automating manufacturing tasks, including assembling, packaging, and labeling products, which allows for:

- Completing tasks with high precision and accuracy is particularly useful for potent medications or where exact dosing is required.
- Inspecting products for defects or quality deviations beyond what the human eye can detect. By using sensors and cameras, robots can identify flaws and reject products that don't meet the required standards.

- Cleaning and sanitizing facilities and equipment to ensure optimal hygiene and reduce the risk of contamination.
- Assuring aseptic conditions by removing operators from the clean environment significantly reduces microbial contamination probability.

This automation can improve efficiency, reduce costs, and enhance quality control.

Robotics can significantly improve pharmaceutical manufacturing by automating repetitive or dangerous tasks while freeing human workers to focus on more complex responsibilities. By doing so, robots can enhance productivity, reduce costs, and improve quality control and safety.

Big Data Analytics

Big data refers to enormous and complex datasets that are difficult to analyze and manage using traditional methods. In pharmaceutical manufacturing, big data can be utilized to monitor and optimize various aspects of the manufacturing process, including process parameters, test results, and quality control. By analyzing data from multiple sources, such as production lines, inventory systems, and distribution networks, big data can help improve manufacturing efficiency, supply chain management, and quality control. Additionally, it can ensure regulatory compliance by tracking and analyzing data from various sources, such as quality control systems, manufacturing processes, and adverse event reporting systems. By utilizing big data, pharmaceutical companies can improve manufacturing efficiency, productivity, and quality control, ultimately leading to better patient outcomes.

Internet of Things (IoT)

The Internet of Things (IoT) is a term used to describe a network of devices that can communicate and exchange data with each other. These devices are equipped with sensors, processors, and connectivity, which enable them to gather and transmit data to other devices and systems.

In pharmaceutical manufacturing, IoT technology can monitor and manage various aspects of the manufacturing process. This approach includes:

- Monitoring manufacturing equipment performance in real-time using IoT sensors, which can detect malfunctions or anomalies. This monitoring can reduce downtime, improve maintenance, and prevent equipment failures.
- Using IoT sensors, tracking the movement of materials and products throughout the supply chain, from raw materials to finished products. This tracking can improve inventory management, reduce waste, and ensure product quality.
- Using IoT sensors to monitor environmental conditions in manufacturing facilities, such as temperature, humidity, and air quality. This monitoring can help ensure that products are manufactured in optimal conditions and that environmental conditions meet regulatory requirements.

- Using real-time monitoring of product quality by tracking parameters such as weight, size, and composition using IoT sensors. This monitoring can help identify defects or quality issues early in manufacturing and prevent non-conforming products from reaching the market.

IoT technology is a powerful tool for improving pharmaceutical manufacturing efficiency, productivity, and quality control. By monitoring and managing various aspects of the manufacturing process in real-time, pharmaceutical companies can optimize operations, reduce costs, and ensure that products meet the highest quality and safety standards.

The Path to Artificial Intelligence

To implement AI in pharmaceutical manufacturing, you need to take several steps. First, identify the manufacturing processes that could benefit from AI and define the problems that need addressing. Next, collect data from various sources such as electronic health records, clinical trial data, production lines, and supply chain systems. Then, integrate the data into a central database that can be accessed and analyzed in real-time.

Afterward, you can apply machine learning algorithms and big data analytics to the collected data to identify patterns, predict outcomes, and optimize processes. For example, machine learning algorithms can identify factors that affect drug efficacy, predict patient outcomes, and optimize manufacturing processes. To extract insights and improve decision-making, implement natural language processing to analyze unstructured data, such as logbooks, lab notebooks, deviations, non-conformances, and batch records.

Use computer vision to analyze images and videos of manufacturing processes to detect defects, optimize production, and ensure product quality. Additionally, integrate IoT sensors and devices into the manufacturing ecosystem to monitor and control various aspects of the process in real-time, such as equipment performance, supply chain management, environmental conditions, and quality control. Finally, implementing robotics to automate repetitive tasks like drug dispensing, packaging, and labeling will improve safety and efficiency.

In summary, implementing AI in pharmaceutical manufacturing involves integrating multiple technologies and systems to create an intelligent and connected ecosystem that can optimize production, improve quality, and reduce costs.

Quality Oversight

Quality oversight is an essential part of using AI in manufacturing. To ensure AI systems work effectively and meet quality standards, here are some best practices: First, integrate AI into existing quality control processes, ensuring that AI is part of the overall quality management system. Next, develop guidelines and standards for the use of AI in manufacturing, including validating and verifying AI algorithms, data use, and personnel training and qualification. Monitoring and auditing AI systems regularly are essential to ensure they perform as intended and produce accurate and reliable data. Incorporating human oversight into AI systems is critical to ensure that AI decisions align with regulatory and quality requirements. This oversight can involve implementing human review and decision-making processes or using transparent and explainable AI systems. Implement data governance processes and quality controls to maintain data integrity and accuracy.

Also, a risk-based approach to quality oversight is crucial, appropriately identifying and managing risks associated with AI technologies. Finally, stay updated with regulatory requirements related to AI in manufacturing, such as guidance from regulatory agencies like the FDA and EMA. The Quality Unit, along with company experts should meet with the FDA CDER's Office of Pharmaceutical Quality (OPQ), which manages the **Emerging Technology Program (ETP)** when developing and implementing AI, not to surprise the FDA after implementation and finding out the implementation missed the mark.

Quality oversight of AI in manufacturing requires a comprehensive approach incorporating AI technologies into existing quality control processes, establishing guidelines and standards, incorporating human oversight and risk management, and staying current with regulatory requirements.

Benefits of AI

When AI is implemented in manufacturing, it can bring countless benefits, such as improving manufacturing processes. For example, it can optimize production planning and quality control, leading to faster production cycles, less downtime, and increased productivity. In addition, AI can detect defects and quality issues in real-time, improving the quality of the products being produced and reducing the risk of defects and recalls. It can also automate dangerous or repetitive tasks, like handling hazardous materials, which reduces the risk of accidents and injuries.

AI can help lower costs in manufacturing by improving efficiency, reducing waste, and optimizing resource allocation. It can analyze enormous amounts of data from various sources to provide insights and support decision-making in product development and supply chain management. AI can monitor equipment performance and predict needed maintenance, reducing downtime and improving maintenance efficiency. AI can also enable customized manufacturing, which allows the production of personalized products tailored to individual patient needs.

Concluding Thoughts on AI

In summary, implementing AI in manufacturing can bring tremendous benefits to manufacturers. By utilizing AI technologies, manufacturers can boost efficiency, reduce costs, and enhance quality. With AI, manufacturers can automate repetitive and mundane tasks, predict equipment maintenance, and optimize all operations. AI is a tool to improve productivity and presents an opportunity to create a better future for the manufacturing industry. Manufacturers must embrace AI and become pioneers in the field, pushing the limits of what is possible and paving the way for a new era of innovation. The potential of AI in manufacturing is limitless, and those who do not adopt it risk being left behind. Now is the time for manufacturers to seize this opportunity, harness the power of AI, and take their operations to new heights.

If done correctly, implementing AI benefits consumers and patients by bringing life-sustaining and lifesaving drugs to market faster. AI can ensure that drugs meet the highest quality standards, providing the highest value for consumers and patients.

I have said from the podium that the future for consumers, families, and patients is bright. On the other hand, those individuals who make up the armies of quality and compliance professionals with companies' quality units are bleak. We should expect significant reductions in the number of quality and compliance professionals required in the future to ensure, maintain, and improve quality and compliance. These professionals must retool their skills if they are to remain relevant.

Chapter 36 - How Pharma 4.0 Will Impact Patients & Quality Professionals

Pharma 4.0 refers to the Fourth Industrial Revolution in the pharmaceutical industry, which involves the integration of digital technologies, automation, and data analytics into pharmaceutical manufacturing and supply chain operations. This integration has significantly changed how quality management systems are designed, implemented, and maintained.

Pharma 4.0 offers quality professionals in the pharmaceutical industry several benefits, such as:

- increased automation and digitization of quality management processes,
- real-time monitoring of production processes and quality metrics,
- greater use of data analytics to identify trends and patterns in quality data,
- improved collaboration and communication between quality professionals and other stakeholders,
- and enhanced supply chain transparency and traceability.

In addition, Pharma 4.0 uses tools and techniques to significantly improve the robustness of the pharmaceutical development, sourcing, manufacturing, and distribution systems, bringing the industry closer to 6 Sigma manufacturing performance, as seen in the electronics and auto industries. Pharmaceutical R&D is crucial in developing and optimizing the manufacturing processes used to produce pharmaceutical products.

Pharma 4.0 also offers several ways to improve the sourcing and manufacturing systems in the pharmaceutical industry.

For example:

- digitalization of the sourcing process,
- blockchain technology for supply chain transparency,
- predictive analytics for demand forecasting, and
- quality management system integration

Can enhance:

- transparency,
- traceability, and
- efficiency in the sourcing process

leading to improved product quality, reduced costs, and greater customer satisfaction.

Similarly, smart manufacturing, predictive maintenance, quality control, advanced analytics, and other technologies enabled by Pharma 4.0 can enhance efficiency and productivity in the manufacturing process. These improvements can lead to improved product quality, reduced waste, and greater efficiency.

Gerry, a friend and mentor, often said, "The industry produces drugs using 3 Sigma performing processes but releases them at 6 Sigma quality levels." This 6 Sigma level is obtained because the products undergo rigorous inspection and testing before being released to ensure they meet the highest quality standards. As a result, the cost of quality in the pharmaceutical industry is around 20 to 25%. These costs are higher than in industries like electronics or auto manufacturing, where products are manufactured using 6 Sigma process, resulting in a cost of quality of around 1 to 3%.

The following chart demonstrates the cost differences between various levels of manufacturing performance.

Manufacturing Performance & Impact on the Cost of Quality

Mfg Perfomance (Sigma)	Defects (ppm)	Yield	Cost of Quality	Estimated Cost of Quality on a Base of $2B
2σ	308537	69.20%	25-35%	$500M-$700M
3σ	66807	93.30%	20-25%	$400M-$500M
4σ	6210	99.40%	12-18%	$240M-$360M
5σ	223	99.98%	4-8%	$80M-$160M
6σ	3.4	99.99966%	1-3%	$20M-$60M

PriceWaterhouseCoopers Presentation, FDA Science Board Meeting November 16, 2001

241

Pharma 4.0 allows the pharmaceutical industry to realize that quality is free. By implementing advanced manufacturing, quality systems, and distribution practices, manufacturers can ensure that products meet the highest quality standards, leading to better and more consistent drugs for patients. These advancements can reduce inspection and testing costs, the risk of recalls or adverse events, and making treatments safer and more effective. In addition, the efficiency of the manufacturing process can be improved, reducing the time it takes to get products to market, which can be particularly beneficial for patients who need life-saving treatments. Overall, Pharma 4.0 has the potential to improve the quality, efficiency, and accessibility of drugs, which will ultimately benefit patients.

Chapter 37 - Quality 4.0

Quality 4.0 is a term that refers to the integration of digital technologies and data analytics into the traditional quality management process to improve product and process quality in the manufacturing industry. Quality 4.0 is part of the larger concept of Industry 4.0, which encompasses the use of digital technologies and data to enhance manufacturing and supply chain processes.

Quality 4.0 can only be achieved by implementing the tools to utilize artificial intelligence effectively.

Overall, Quality 4.0 represents a significant shift in how manufacturers approach quality management, leveraging digital technologies and data analytics to achieve higher quality and operational efficiency.

As mentioned earlier, Industry and Quality 4.0 hold a bright future for consumers, families, and patients. On the other hand, those individuals who make up the armies of quality and compliance professionals within companies' quality units are bleak. We should expect significant reductions in the number of quality and compliance professionals required in the future to ensure, maintain, and improve quality and compliance when advanced techniques are deployed to protect patients.

These professionals must retool their skills if they are to remain relevant.

Chapter 38 - Conclusions

In summary, being an effective and great-quality leader requires

- **If Necessary, Put Your Job On The Line:** Sometimes, a quality professional may have to make the hardest decision – to protect patients at all costs, even if it means putting their job on the line. Putting patients first, even if it means risking your career, requires a solid moral compass and a commitment to ethical principles. Ultimately, the role of a quality professional is to serve as a patient advocate, ensuring that the care provided is of the highest quality and safety.

- **Study And Learn From Experts And The Legends Of Quality:** I mentioned several experts I studied while honing my quality skills, such as Deming, Juran, Toyota, and Ford. This knowledge gave me the base to build on to understand the relationship between quality and capacity, manufacturing, and satisfying the customer, allowing me to be more effective in convincing others of the value of a modern quality system.

- **SWIPE Is An Acronym For Steal With Integrity and Pride from Everywhere:** It's a process of making improvements across an organization without waiting for people to reinvent the wheel. By SWIPEing ideas, initiatives, and procedures from successful organizations via publications, conferences, networking, and benchmarking. SWIPEing creates quicker and more accessible results, as the intellectual component of the work has already been completed.

- **Do What Is In The Best Interest Of Patients:** Using the patient as your North Star makes doing the right things easy and straightforward.

- **Embrace Sales And Marketing Sills:** Promoting quality within a pharmaceutical company ensures that products are safe, effective, and high-quality. It also helps to create a quality culture, ensure compliance with regulations and standards, and identify and mitigate risks.

- **Focus On Quality Versus Compliance:** Focusing on quality and insisting on having significant product knowledge, robust and repeatable manufacturing processes, well-designed control procedures, and continuously monitoring and improving the process will prevent non-conformances, defects, product failures, product complaints, and recalls. Thus, quality will ensure a significant level of compliance.

- **Make It Easy To Comply.** Making it easy to comply was always a challenge throughout my career because individuals with good intentions would implement requirements that were hard to follow and make jobs harder. I can't stress enough the importance of helping individuals comply by making it easy to comply.

- **Implement Bold Initiatives Where Required:** There are times when bold initiatives are necessary, completely reinventing a failing system or implementing a system that is missing. My only words of caution when implementing big, bold initiatives are to try to implement them in small, achievable steps, building on the success of each step.

- **Do What Is Necessary To "Connect The Dots:"** Connecting the dots relates to finding connections between seemingly unrelated ideas or information. Connecting the dots allows you to predict events impacting the organization and implement programs that are consistently more effective and efficient before you are forced to do so.

- **Persistence And Determination:** The essential trait of successful quality professions is not giving up when the majority says "No Way." Determination is the drive to achieve a goal, while persistence is the ability to keep going despite setbacks and obstacles. These qualities are essential for achieving any goal, whether it is in business, sports, or personal development. Persistence and determination are important qualities for quality professionals because they enable them to tackle challenges, strive for continuous improvement, maintain attention to detail, pursue long-term goals, and drive positive change within their organizations.

- **Do Not Ignore The Supply Chain:** The supply chain is critical in ensuring product and service quality. It involves the entire process of sourcing raw materials, components, and services, all the way to delivering the final product to the end consumer. A well-managed and efficient supply chain can significantly impact the overall quality of the product or service.

Epilogue

I am happy to report today that I am free of cancer. My kidney surgery was successful. I had the opportunity to see how our healthcare system works in real-time.

During a routine CT Scan, there was an incidental finding of a 1.5mm tumor on my right kidney. In discussions with a urologist, we decided the best approach was to remove the tumor and part of my right kidney using robotic surgery and that we would wait until after my 40th Wedding Anniversary celebration with the family.

On July 11, 2023, I entered the Mayo Clinic in Jacksonville, Florida, for my surgery. I was lucky to be the first surgery of the day. While in recovery, I received promising news that surgery went well. During my two-night stay, I received intravenous fluids and numerous medications. While at Mayo, I saw firsthand how my care team always did what was in my best interests (the patient), from the doctors, physician assistants, nurses, and pharmacists team to housekeeping. Five days later, I received a call from my urologist informing me that the pathology report was good and that the tumor was malignant, but the margins of the tumor and part of the removed kidney were free of cancer. Therefore, I was cancer free, and I would not need chemo. I will be monitored every six months via a Chest X-ray and MRI for multiple years.

I feel blessed because:

- The tumor was found "incidentally" before I had any symptoms during a CT Scan for something different
- I had access to excellent medical care
- I was not impacted by quality problems or drug shortages
- I have a fantastic support structure consisting of colleagues, friends, and family.
- My post-surgery set of six-month follow-up scans confirmed that I am **Cancer-Free**!

My 40-year career working with pharmaceuticals and medical devices has been rewarding, non-stop, and exciting. I had the opportunity to meet many wonderful people across the globe, from Politicians like Congressmen, Senators, Members of Parliament, and Policymakers in numerous Agencies, Regulators, Non-Government Organizations, Healthcare Professionals, Patients, and Consumers. I have testified in the U.S. House of Representatives and U.S. Senate on supply chain security, drug shortages, and non-profit drug companies. In addition, I had meetings inside The White House and at the United Nations. My travels took me to too many countries to list. However, it was fascinating visiting Cuba and China. Finally, I made hundreds of presentations at professional and trade organizations' meetings or conferences.

Thinking back on my family, recreational activities, and business demands, I wonder when I ever had time to sleep. I never missed a softball game, theater performance, or important family event. To meet my family commitments and excel at work, I woke up early and worked before the kids got up and then worked late into the night after the kids went to bed.

The Roller Coaster

I opened with a famous poem called "The Train." I will close with a poem I authored, "The Roller Coaster."

The job of a quality executive, Is like a roller coaster ride.
It's full of twists and turns, And high stakes to abide.
The journey can be fast-paced, With deadlines to be met.
New challenges to be faced, And new opportunities to get.
There's a constant sense of movement, A drive to always improve.
With new technologies to explore, And new processes to groove.
Just like a roller coaster, The ride can be quite scary.
Mistakes can have consequences, Which can be quite contrary.
But with teamwork and dedication, The ride can be quite thrilling.
And the quality executive can feel, A sense of achievement fulfilling.
So hold on tight and enjoy the ride, Of being a quality executive.
It's like a roller coaster journey, Full of excitement and incentive.

Made in the USA
Columbia, SC
17 September 2024